Greg O'Connor has studied Aikido and other martial arts for over twenty-five years. He is one of the few full-time professional certified Aikido instructors in the world. He is the founder and chief instructor of Aikido Centers of New Jersey and Aikido Centers, Inc. and co-founder of Aikido Schools of New Jersey. He is the author of other books and articles on Aikido including *The Aikido Student Handbook*.

The *Elements of* is a series designed to present high quality introductions to a broad range of essential subjects.

The books are commissioned specifically from experts in their fields. They provide readable and often unique views of the various topics covered, and are therefore of interest both to those who have some knowledge of the subject, as well as to those who are approaching it for the first time.

Many of these concise yet comprehensive books have practical suggestions and exercises which allow personal experience as well as theoretical understanding, and offer a valuable source of information on many important themes.

In the same series

the elements of

aikido

greg o'connor

ELEMENT

Shaftesbury, Dorset • Boston, Massachusetts • Melbourne, Victoria

© Element Books Limited 1998
Text and illustrations © Greg O'Connor 1998

First published in Great Britain in 1998 by
Element Books Limited
Shaftesbury, Dorset SP7 8BP

Published in the USA in 1998 by
Element Books, Inc.
160 North Washington St, Boston, MA 02114

Published in Australia in 1998 by
Elements Books
and distributed by Penguin Australia Ltd
487 Maroondah Highway, Ringwood, Victoria, 3134

Cover design by Max Fairbrother
Design by Roger Lightfoot
Typeset by WestKey Limited, Falmouth, Cornwall
Printed and bound in Great Britain by
Biddles Ltd, Guildford and King's Lynn

British Library Cataloguing in Publication
data available

Library of Congress Cataloging in Publication
data available

ISBN 1-86204-322-1

CONTENTS

LIST OF ILLUSTRATIONS

This book is dedicated to those who have the extraordinary strength to seek peace.

ACKNOWLEDGEMENTS

I would like to thank the many friends who contributed their typing and editorial assistance, as well as their commentaries, to the production of this book. In particular I would like to thank Les Babish and Larry Bieri who generously volunteered their time, knowledge and editing skills. Also, special thanks to Stan Pranin for his help on historical accuracies.

I want to thank my wife, Mary Kay, for all her invaluable help and enthusiastic support of this project, as well as my/our work in life and in Aikido, and to thank all my students for their support and understanding. This book is a gift of love to them as well as to the world.

Finally, I wish to thank all my teachers – the obvious and the not so. I still have a lot to learn.

FOREWORD

I am privileged to write this foreword for Greg O'Connor's book.

The Elements of Aikido is not only geared towards Aikido practitioners, but it will be widely beneficial for people interested in *budo* (martial ways) in general. Almost 35 years ago I came to New York City to introduce and spread Aikido. At that time there were only a handful of books published on the subject of *budo*, written by Japanese martial arts experts. Most of these books, including my own, focused predominantly on the technical aspects of the respective martial art of the author. Rarely were the spiritual or philosophical elements of *budo* discussed; rather, we stressed the details of technique.

Nowadays there are quite a lot of books on martial arts written by Westerners. Obviously these writings portray a different angle or point of view from our works in the past. I believe these contemporary works to be informed and insightful, not to mention accessible to the public through ease of understanding. For that reason I am grateful to Greg O'Connor for producing this book. I truly hope that *The Elements of Aikido* gives people both inside and outside Aikido a better understanding of what the art really is.

Aikido is a wonderful art! We participate in it not only to improve our physical condition or our proficiency as a martial artist, but also for the enjoyment we gain from its graceful movement and its meditative aspects. We engage in Aikido practice to improve self-discipline and mind–body co-ordination, and to increase our spiritual awareness. One of the most reassuring factors is that no matter who you are or what field you are in, Aikido will be beneficial to your career, your home life and your personal development as a whole.

Yoshimitsu Yamada

8th dan, Chairman of The United States Aikido Federation
Chief Instructor of The New York Aikikai

INTRODUCTION

This book presents an overview of the extraordinarily rich martial way of Aikido.

There are many excellent books on Aikido available today. Some briefly cover its history, philosophy and basic techniques; some give extensive details about the founder of Aikido, Morihei Ueshiba, covering his life and his words, and the history and roots behind the development of his art. Many works address Aikido's unique philosophical and ethical approaches and document its more esoteric, spiritual and cultural roots. Many give an introduction to Aikido's various approaches, styles and tremendous range of technique, with explanatory examples as well as excellent, and extensive, photographic documentation. These are especially helpful when someone is already practising the art. The Aikido student can use these books as reference material for further clarification on the techniques to which they may already have been exposed in an Aikido class under the guidance of a qualified teacher. Still others relate how Aikido's principles can be applied more directly to everyday personal interactions, so improving the quality of daily living. Some provide a guide as to how Aikido principles may reduce stress and improve everything from conflict resolution skills to leadership skills. Aikido, as all these elements indicate, has a great deal to offer.

Because of its diversity, trying to describe Aikido is akin to trying to describe all of nature, or to explain the universe. This is not so outrageous a statement as it sounds since, as you will see, Aikido requires one to embrace both nature and the universe. Aikido is so abundant in what it has to offer both the individual and society that no one book could ever contain its enormity. Nonetheless, with this in mind, I will introduce you to Aikido's depth and breadth. After that the journey is up to you.

NOTE   Japanese terminology makes no distinction between singular and plural. The word *dojo* (training space), for instance, can refer to either a single *dojo* or many.

1 • WHAT IS AIKIDO?

*. . . listen to the voice of Aikido. It is not for correcting others;
it is for correcting your own mind.*
— The founder of Aikido, Morihei Ueshiba

AIKIDO DEFINED

Aikido is a martial art for lovers. Lovers of peace. It requires
that you love yourself, that you love others, the good and not
so, that you love the ground you walk on, the air you breathe,
the dog who digs up your garden and the stars that beckon
infinity. Aikido's magical techniques, its miraculous results
and its use of the mysterious cosmic forces that we all possess have given it a mystical reputation, and deservedly so. It
is in a class of its own among the martial arts. It has at its core
a unique philosophical approach for a martial art: that the
attacker must be cared for. The paradox of Aikido is that it is
potentially lethal yet benevolently peaceful. Despite its real
capabilities as a devastating method of self-defence, it is a
system whose powerful techniques are mastered only
through the pursuit of non-violence.

Aikido is beautiful to watch and even more rewarding to
perform. To the uninitiated, Aikido is seen as a predominantly throwing and pinning art where one blends with an
attack instead of clashing with it. The attacker's strength,

1

momentum and energy are used to redirect the attack into dynamic projections or simple, yet effective, controlling pins. All the techniques in Aikido move one's partner in a natural manner. Because of the ethics of the art, the bends of the body and its joints are merely accentuated in a natural direction, allowing redirection and control without injury. If any minor pain is inflicted, it is merely for motivational purposes and as soon as the technique is released, any discomfort or pain disappears. Aikido's principles and ethics are such that if we *do* injure someone it simply is *not* good Aikido. In fact, I will go so far as to say, it is not *true* Aikido.

Aikido is based on co-operation, mutual respect and friendship. Aikido is finesse – not force. Its philosophy, ideals and ethics are inseparable from the actual training. Its practice develops a strong, yet supple, relaxed body as well as a calm, clear mind, providing an inner peace which can then be passed on to others.

Those who are attracted to Aikido wish to be able to protect themselves, as well as others, easily and effectively, without resorting to the use of violence. Aikido's circular flowing techniques are fun, effective, and can be learned by anyone regardless of size, age, gender or athletic ability. Men, women and children all find Aikido appealing because its techniques are not based on pitting one's strength against another's. It is an art for anyone who seeks to be at peace with themselves and their surroundings.

As a martial art, Aikido gives one the ability to defend oneself without resorting to aggression. Concentration, awareness and focusing power are greatly enhanced while allowing for balance and calmness to be maintained in all situations. A healthy self-esteem, a clear head and a sound body are the result. This state of being is then naturally carried off the mat and into the activity of daily life.

The practitioner begins with a calm, balanced state of mind, body and spirit; in a state of peace. As an attack comes in, the Aikido practitioner, or *aikidoka*, maintains this state of being while adjusting and blending with the attack. The *aikidoka* can then redirect the attack safely away and into a variety of throws and pins while remaining fully aware of the opportunities for striking and retaliation, which present themselves within the openings created by the Aikido technique. Despite these opportunities, the *aikidoka* chooses to exercise the more peaceful, non-violent resolution in completing the defence. The *aikidoka* can, if needed in a real life-and-death situation, perform any of Aikido's throws and pins with severe consequences. However, because of the preferred non-violence of the philosophy, the *aikidoka* trains to exercise the more ethical approach of every technique's capabilities. In the founder's words, 'Aikido is the loving protection of all things'. In essence, this means that Aikido is a method of protection for all beings, protection of the transgressor as well as the transgressed. In his words, 'it is a way to reconcile the world'.

Aikido is the word that Morihei Ueshiba eventually used to describe his new martial art. It is a combination of Japanese concepts and can be translated to mean 'The Way of Uniting Ki Spirit'. The premise of Aikido is to blend with an opponent's energy and spirit and redirect the attack safely away, resulting in no harm coming to the *aikidoka* and, ideally, even to the attacker. It is circular and fluid in its techniques as opposed to linear, harsh and static, which I will talk more about later in this book.

Aikido is not a religion or a religious pursuit and it holds to no religious doctrine. It is, however, a spiritual path. Therefore, because of the attention Aikido gives to both individual and universal spirit, it can be, and is, practised comfortably and enthusiastically by people everywhere, and by people of many religions.

Aikido is, of course, a powerful method of self-defence – a martial art. However, paradoxically, it is one that is an alternative to violence. Its techniques have a unique range of application, from soft to severe. Joints are not broken, although if the situation warrants it they could be. One who wishes to master Aikido prefers not to hurt.

Indeed, some say it is a method of learning how to kill. To some extent this may be true, because it is only through learning what *can* kill that one can exercise the option and the choice *not* to kill. All Aikido techniques, if applied poorly and irresponsibly, can be potentially dangerous and even deadly. However, Aikido's unique ethics offer alternatives to that undesirable option.

Practitioners of Aikido often describe it as a powerful method of self-exploration. They might even say that it is a cohesive method of holistic integration. It can be defined further as a meditative art where one develops a deep calm that is incorporated into all activities. Poetically, Aikido is a dynamic and exhilarating art where one dances in the flash and flow of energy. Socially, it is a method of conflict resolution resulting in a 'win-win' scenario; winner/winner rather than winner/loser, and victor/victor rather than victor/vanquished.

Aikido is beautiful to watch. Its movements are fluid and dance-like; its results incredible. It can be unbelievable: explosive, magical, and so complicated in its simplicity. Everything in nature is contained in Aikido: the lightness of air; the solidity of earth and rock; the adaptability of water; the sting of fire; the blinding shock of lightning; the unending resonance of thunder. Aikido can be as soft and comforting as a sun-warmed breeze or as decisive and complete as a grizzly bear attack. Aikido can be performed with the power of a crashing wave or the passiveness of an autumn leaf drifting away from its branch. All the elements and characteristics of nature are found in Aikido. Its power is from the universe that is both in us and around us. There is no separation from everything else. For those of us who are addicted to its practice, this is its appeal.

BUDO & BUJITSU

Aikido is a *budo*, meaning literally, 'martial way'. The prefix *bu* refers to martial characteristics. The suffix *do* means 'way of' or 'path', and refers more to the internal or spiritual aspects pursued through the practice of those particular martial techniques. *Budo*, which became the ideal discipline that all samurai followed, was a code of honour that can be compared to the code of chivalry of medieval knights. The suffix *jitsu*, when added to *bu* to become *bujitsu*, means

4

'martial combat' and refers to martial techniques practised for the battlefield or combat purposes. Another way of looking at it would be to say that *bujitsu* is a way that emphasizes the outward combat technique as a means of killing; whereas *budo* emphasizes the inward combat for self-purification and as a means of living. Aikido is then classified as a *budo* because it stresses internal development as opposed to only its combat effectiveness.

Aikido's founder came to believe that true *budo* has no enemies – it is the pursuit of a peace which, at its core, has a deep love and respect for everyone and everything. True *budo*, he believed, should not destroy, but should nurture and protect all beings. True *budo* is for the fostering of life, not the taking of it.

AIKIDO & OTHER MARTIAL ARTS

Martial artists have spent a thousand years perfecting both their internal and external balance. They have studied diligently to develop special skills that would enable them to meet life and its challenges in a relaxed, but alert and composed manner. They have sought to acquire the ability to respond quickly, effortlessly and with maximum efficiency in all situations. They have searched for an ideal art that would give them these capabilities. Aikido is such an art.

Most martial arts are based on the theory of self-protection and preservation. Aikido is based on the insistence of not only *mutual* protection and preservation, but also mutual growth and enhancement. Like most martial arts, it begins and ends with respect; but Aikido takes that a step further. It requires that the respect be maintained at a high level – throughout the interaction and even beyond – to all things at all times.

The main goal of most martial arts is to vanquish a foe. Wise leaders warn us, though, that a vanquished foe is still a dangerous one. Revenge and retribution are reactions common to us all. Even if our opponent has been completely destroyed, we may produce these desires in others, who may have been emotionally affected by our actions or who simply disagreed with us on their use. There are always going to be those that disagree with us and our actions – so why create even more?

Aikido's founder believed that it is not a technique to fight and defeat an enemy. It is a way to reconcile the world and make human beings one family.' Aikido seeks the harmonius resolution of conflict in all its varied forms. It is a strategy for winning that, ideally, has no losers. It requires one to remain centered and balanced on all levels so as to recognize any attack, blend with it, and redirect it into a safe conclusion for all.

It is primarily a defensive martial art, preferring mainly defensive strategies. However, it can certainly be used, if necessary, to take the initiative once an attack is imminent. If moral judgement indicates an offensive response to deal with an attack, then Aikido easily has that capability. Many *aikidoka* may cringe at that statement, insisting that peace be maintained in all circumstances. I fully agree that this is the preferred ideal. But the additional reality is that there are predators in the world who would not only victimize you, but also your loved ones. Would you not rush to their defence without a second thought? Many people would because the protective instinct is a powerful one and it can be a potent ally. Since Aikido is an art of protection it can draw on that natural instinct to qualify its use and response. It gives credence to our protective nature and, with guidance, allows it to flourish.

In Aikido there is no attack *per se*. There are no aggressive strategies. We point out the openings and opportunities, known as *suki*, where strikes and kicks can be applied or executed. These are created during the actual execution of the Aikido technique itself. Knowing one has the option to take a more offensive approach at any point should give one confidence to be able to choose more ethical options to dispel the conflict. We also teach the new student how to execute a proper punch, strike, kick or grab in order to properly defend against them. However, we do not drill in those strikes or kicks. In arts that rely on offensive striking, practitioners are put through solitary kicking and punching drills, performing the same punch or kick over and over again. This is done so as to not only perfect its execution, but to make it second nature. The majority of the practice is spent repeating the same kick or strike hundreds of times, then moving on to practise another kick or punch in the same manner. It is interesting that a great many of the people that come to Aikido have already been through another art, usually one of the striking arts. They often wish to expand their horizons, either martially or morally, and have no need or desire to perform such drills.

In Aikido, as a basic practice, a single attack is performed and a specific Aikido technique is demonstrated by the instructor as a response against it. The students practise by repeating the entire sequence, alternating both left and right sides to develop symmetry, balance and ambidexterity.

Some other arts can be considered linear and static, insisting on maintaining one's position regardless of the force coming in. Attacks are blocked and deflected. In order to effectively perform those blocks conditioning of the forearms and shins is needed, resulting in tissue bruising and damage, calluses, calcium build-ups on the bone from hairline fracturing, and general trauma of the body. Aikido does not require such conditioning.

In Aikido, the attack is not blocked, but blended with. It is not deflected; it is redirected. Force is not met with direct force. We blend with the attack's force, adding our own balanced energy to it and sending it safely by us. We can describe Aikido as being non-linear, circular and fluid. We maintain our position by moving it. Our body movement, not our body, absorbs the power of the attack. When the attack comes in, the aikidoist envelops it, at the same time adjusting safely to a new position while guiding the passing attack safely away.

Other arts may also use similar principles (ie absorption and redirection) but often conclude the interaction with the more violent options of striking or kicking. Some have only limited interaction with a live practice partner and some not at all, preferring solitary practice, but in Aikido you *must* practise with a partner. Aikido requires personal interaction with its various degrees of commitment and intensity. Just as you cannot learn to ride a horse without the horse, you cannot learn to blend Aikido technique to another's attack without that other person. You must see the other person before you; you must feel his or her presence, and how it affects your heart.

Other martial art systems are typically competition based. They have contests and tournaments where qualities of assertion and fortitude are brought out and developed. These qualities represent the healthy side of competition. The down side is that overemphasis on competition may develop into aggression. Assertion is desirable. Aggression is not. It can lead one to the assumption that 'might makes right' or 'to get what you want you have to fight'. This may also lead to the belief that you must defeat someone else in order to achieve your goals. In Aikido we strive for a more evolved approach. Through principles based on respect, co-operation and benevolence Aikido strives for mutual benefits resulting from any interaction. Using Aikido, we are hoping to have learned something from the struggles of those who have gone before us; something that not only allows us to survive as individuals, but also as a responsible and continually evolving species.

Other arts pit the practitioner against one solitary opponent. These contests, being essentially sports contests, require participants to follow specific rules, necessary for safety and good sportsmanship. Because of this the full range of the opponent's attack capabilities and options is restricted. They are sports contests where a sort of gentlemen's Marquis of Queensbury rules apply. In a real-life physical assault there is no such thing as sportsmanship. These sport combatants do not have to be concerned with such things as unnecessary roughness, biting, vitals being viciously attacked, eyes being gouged out, the introduction of weapons, or additional attackers coming at them simultaneously.

Traditional Aikido, as conceived by Morihei Ueshiba, has no contests, competitions or tournaments. Some Aikido styles, such as Tomiki style, do have competition. That may be fine for those who wish to compete but, nevertheless, it is contrary to the basic philosophy of traditional Aikido.

The competition that traditional Aikido encourages is the one that endeavours to improve upon and evolve our own characters, to balance ourselves, and to correct and refine our own behaviour patterns. The founder of Aikido said that it was not an art for correcting others, but for correcting our own minds. The battle is not with an outside enemy, but with the inner demons that work to prevent us from living a life of deep fulfilment and contentment − a life of true peace. The competition is in the challenge to balance ourselves on all levels − physical, mental, emotional and spiritual − regardless of the situations in which we find ourselves. The challenge is also to accomplish all this on our own merit, not at the expense of damaging another's health or well-being, or resorting to the defeat of someone else; destruction and violence are undesirable alternatives. The ideal result of Aikido training is to simultaneously better ourselves and others, whether they are attackers or supporters.

The rules contained within competition restrict an opponent's full options, limit the contest to one attacker, and foster a certain level of complacency. This is something that can be very detrimental in a real-life attack. With Aikido training we assume the attacker is not going to 'stick to the rules'. Using any of our Aikido techniques in an actual self-defence scenario, we must be able to neutralize one attacker and still use them to effectively shield against any further attackers. All this is done while retaining the option to throw one attacker into the others in order to stop or impede them.

In an actual life-and-death confrontation the attacker can, and often will, resort to any means at hand to ensure success. Your resourcefulness and self-defence abilities determine the outcome. This means that you, as an aikidoist, must be constantly vigilant throughout your performance of the Aikido technique. You must remain alert for any opportunities your partner may have. They can execute additional strikes or grabs, introduce weapons, or be joined by others helping in the attack. Therefore, as abilities advance, the aikidoist must be aware of not only one partner's full capabilities but also the possibility of multiple attackers; and to still neutralize those attempts easily, efficiently and ethically.

Though practised as a martial art with these critical martial points in mind, the ultimate idea of Aikido is to bring people together. To create calm out of chaos; to find our common condition, to break down our feelings of separateness from one another and, in doing so, also break down our feelings of separateness from everything.

Typically, many who are attracted to Aikido have already experienced competition. They may no longer seek the forum of one-on-one contests to define or enhance their characters. Contests and competitions are very good, of course, for developing such qualities as determination, tenacity, teamwork and fair play. Aikido develops these same qualities but in an alternative context, with the most intimidating foe any of us will ever face – our own psyche. It is our own psyche's patterns of conduct that can keep us from enjoying a peaceful and happy life.

In Aikido training you work with men and women – big, small, strong, weak, scared and scary. You have to recognize what each unique individual does to your internal equilibrium; what effect their presence, mood, energy level, personality and so on have on you; how they affect the interaction and outcome when practising the various Aikido techniques.

Many other martial arts have what can be loosely described to as a 'boot camp' atmosphere with a militaristic approach to training. The discipline can be harsh and even severe. This, like a training camp, certainly has the effect of forging character, developing perseverance and individual will-power. It can enhance personal discipline, increase individual tenacity and fortitude, implant respect and adherence to authority, and impart the advantages of teamwork. The advantage of Aikido training is that it includes these very same benefits. With Aikido, however, they are brought about by alternative methods involving co-operation and compassion – and in an alternative context based on friendship and peaceful camaraderie.

10

Many of the people who find Aikido attractive do not need or desire training camp methods. They may have, as the saying goes, 'been there, seen it, done it, got the T-shirt'. Some have even had extensive experience, attained significant rank in another discipline, and wish to move on to expand their horizons. Commonly, many do not feel the need to prove anything to anyone else and wish to enrich themselves in other ways.

'True victory,' Aikido's founder said, 'is victory over self.' If you can claim that victory and bask in its glow then you have already won over every other opponent and situation that will come before you. This is a very real challenge, as we all know, because this type of victory is only attained after meeting and accepting the challenge of all challenges: to maintain our composure, our balance, our peace, as often as possible, if not always. In Aikido, this victory – to be able to use that state of balance to act with evolved appropriateness – is the goal and the reward.

Although I have researched, studied and experienced various other martial arts, as an Aikido instructor I may tend to give a biased opinion. The best way to find out what is best for you is to do just what you are doing now: read about the martial arts. Seek out a teacher and a school (see Chapter 9) that is a reputable representation of that art. When deciding to study any martial art you should be comfortable knowing that it is the best one for you. Knowing what the various other arts offer, and determining what most appeals to you, will go a long way to increase the dedication and focus you will need to muster and maintain for your training, whatever art you choose. Should you choose to study Aikido, your research may give you a greater understanding, interest and appreciation.

2 · A BRIEF HISTORY OF AIKIDO

The secret of Aikido is to harmonize with the movement of the universe and bring ourselves into accord with the universe itself. He who has gained the secret of Aikido has the universe in himself and can say 'I am the universe'.

– Morihei Ueshiba

Aikido was created by Morihei Ueshiba, a renowned Japanese martial arts master, as a way of combining his formidable martial capabilities with his deep spiritual pursuits.

Master Ueshiba was born in the small fishing village of Tanabe on the eastern coast of Japan in 1883. As a young boy he witnessed his father being roughed up by local hoodlums and he was powerless to come to his aid. Even though he was a small and sickly child, this experience added to his resolve that he would develop himself to become strong in both body and spirit. He began to study many martial arts including *jujitsu*, *kenjitsu*, *jojitsu*, *sojutsu* and *sumo*, as well as various other sword and staff arts. As years passed he became nationally known for his extraordinary abilities as a martial arts master. His art took many names over the early years of its development, among which were *Aiki-budo* and *Ueshiba Ryu-Aikijujitsu*.

12

Figure 1   The founder of Aikido, Morihei Ueshiba

Morihei was of small stature, even for a typical Japanese, standing just under 5ft tall. He trained himself so relentlessly and thoroughly, though, that he became physically very imposing and extremely strong. His feats of strength became quite remarkable and well known. For example, there are accounts where he was able to move stones so large that four or five people together could not move the same stone. He also sought to forge and strengthen his spirit, and made a life-time study of the martial arts. To this day stories of his superhuman feats and almost magical powers abound. Although he was to gain a reputation for being virtually unbeatable, he was, at the same time, profoundly troubled with the conflict that arose between his martial skills and his spiritual pursuits.

All his life, the founder was a deeply spiritual man on a deeply spiritual search. Like the majority of Japanese he was exposed to zen, Buddhism and Shinto beliefs. Shinto is a religion native to Japan and practised by most Japanese, and is also a belief system that does not negate other beliefs. Many Japanese, for instance, practise both Buddhism and Shintoism. Thus when Morihei encountered a religion by the name of Omoto-Kyo he was able to embrace its beliefs fully, and then dedicate his life to its practice.

Omoto-Kyo was founded by Nao Deguchi, a humble peasant woman, who was, reportedly, a healer and who had a gift of clairvoyance. Meeting Onisaburo Deguchi, the then current leader of Omoto-Kyo, had a profound effect on Morihei. It was Onisaburo Deguchi who told Morihei that, because of his extraordinary abilities, he should open a *dojo* and teach his martial art. This he did and dedicated himself to his calling, that of pursuing and combining his spiritual and martial paths.

One of the basic principles of Omoto-Kyo was the aspect of *kotodama*, the belief of sound being the creative force of the universe. The *kotodama* range of octaves, from deep to high pitch tones, could be arranged as such in chants that one could vocalize. Then, with the various vibrations generated, one could, ideally, energize the body, mind and spirit and connect it all to the entire cosmos. Morihei therefore incorporated the sounds of *kotodama* into his own life, practice and purification rituals. This, according to his words, was what connected him to God.

As time went on and Morihei Ueshiba's martial abilities became quite well known he was regularly confronted by other accomplished martial artists seeking to better him. He would always easily defeat these challengers, and as years passed he became weary of them, finding no satisfaction or joy in repeatedly defeating them. One such encounter with yet another insistent challenger would bring about a profound life change for Ueshiba.

The challenger, in this case, was a naval officer. Reluctantly, Morihei accepted his challenge and invited the naval officer to strike him, using a wooden sword. Morihei easily avoided the repeated attempts to hit him, and when the challenger finally grew frustrated, tired and spent, Morihei left him and entered a nearby garden. While there he had what he described as an experience of enlightenment where he was bathed in a golden light. He said it was at that moment that the realization that 'I am the universe' came into him; it was then that the true meaning of *budo*, the martial way, was revealed to him. The revelation was that true *budo* was for the love and protection of all things. This brought him to the realization and solidification of his life purpose and revealed to him the path to combine his spiritual awareness with his martial method. This wisdom contributed to the further evolution of his art which would become Aikido; we may even go so far as to say that this was the true birth of Aikido. He knew then that winning at someone else's expense was not really winning, and that the only true victory was the victory over the conflict within ourselves. This discord is the greatest adversary in our lives. The highest skill levels that can be achieved are needed to attain this victory. This, indeed, is 'fighting the good fight' on the most difficult battlefield.

It was some time after he had this experience that his art came to be known as Aikido. Aikido, economically translated, means the way to love and harmony with the spirit of all things. When broken down more literally *ai* can be translated as 'love/harmony', *ki* is 'spirit/energy/life force' and *do* means 'way of' or 'path'.

Because of the awe and reverence they felt for Master Ueshiba, his students began referring to him respectfully as O Sensei, which means 'Great Teacher'. This is how he is referred to today by Aikido practitioners all over the world.

O Sensei, in explaining Aikido, often referred to the phrase *take-musu aiki* (see horizontal *kanji* on front cover by O Sensei). *Take-musu aiki* means, roughly, that Aikido is the martial way of unending rebirth and rejuvenation with limitless and boundless creativity. It is *misogi*, purification. Through the practice of Aikido one continually renews oneself through that purification process.

He felt that martial artists who only practised combat techniques were short-sighted in their true value; that in acquiring the ability to take life, they should also develop the power to give life. He felt that winning at someone else's cost was not truly winning at all, and that true victory was winning over oneself and one's own demons. He came to realize that physical force could not possibly win over the power of a spirit rooted and connected to the divine spirit. Throughout his years O Sensei's teaching of Aikido was filled with references to the divine, and how his Aikido connected him to

15

God and revealed the true natures of both himself and the universe.

He often used references to obscure Japanese mythology with which even his Japanese students were unfamiliar. He spoke metaphorically of the sword that takes life and the sword that gives life. Literally speaking, an actual sword can be used to kill, yet it can be used wisely to protect and preserve righteousness. The impetuous and the fearful draw the sword easily. The sword that remains sheathed remains there only by the fearlessness, wisdom and strength of character of its owner. Metaphorically speaking, the sword that kills also destroys its master. The sword that gives life is used to cut through our own ego and selfishness, and opens us to the reality that we all share. O Sensei, therefore, admonished that 'Aikido is not for correcting others. It is a tool for correcting and polishing your own mind'.

Most are familiar with the advice of Jesus Christ when he said, 'He that lives by the sword, dies by the sword'. This is the same advice the founder of Aikido would offer. This death is not so much a physical death, but an internal one: a spiritual death. O Sensei said, 'When an enemy tries to fight with me, the universe itself, he has to break the harmony of the universe. Hence, at the moment he has the mind to fight with me, he is already defeated.' We refer to those that lose as such because they have indeed lost; they have lost something of importance to them, something of value. The most important thing we can lose is our sense of peace and contentment. We value our own serenity. True serenity comes from loving and supporting the world around and in us and, hopefully, having it returned in kind. In using violence, or when winning at the expense of another, we lose. We have lost our connection with universal harmony. We have lost our serenity.

Violence is an act of desperation that often has its beginnings in frustration and pain. The reliance on violence harms the one committing it as well – either immediately or ultimately. In such a situation such people have lost the ability to control themselves, and to see other options. They have lost their sense of personal power and dignity. They have lost peace. They have lost love.

If your character, personal resolve and capacity for compassion are strong enough, there is no need to use violence. One knows that violence is a knife that cuts both ways. One can choose to have the wisdom and intelligence to explore more productive, and therefore more desirable, alternatives. These alternatives should benefit all.

O Sensei realized that the people of the world needed the help that Aikido could bring; and so, in the 1950s and early '60s he encouraged some of his students to live and teach abroad. Today Aikido can be found in nearly every country and practically every major city in the world.

O Sensei developed two *dojo* which remain active today. The main *dojo* is in the Shinjuku section of Tokyo, and is referred to as *Aikido Hombu Dojo*, or Aikido home *dojo*. It continues today as World Headquarters for Aikido. Since O Sensei's passing in 1969, Aikido Hombu Dojo and The International Aikido Federation are headed by O Sensei's son, Kisshomaru Ueshiba, who, in Aikido terms, is referred to as *Doshu* or 'leader of the way'. Kisshomaru's son, and O Sensei's grandson, Moriteru, is the current *dojo cho*, or *dojo* administrator, for Aikido Hombu Dojo.

O Sensei's other *dojo* is located in the Japanese countryside town of Iwama in Ibaraki Prefecture. The Iwama *dojo* also contains the Aiki Shrine, or *Aiki Jinja*, which was built and dedicated by O Sensei to the spirit of Aikido. The Iwama *dojo* was very special to O Sensei for it was there that he was able to devote himself to his gardening. Working with the earth, nurturing and growing his plants provided a communication with nature that O Sensei valued a great deal. He felt that his gardening and his Aikido were intertwined. Morihiro Saito Sensei, having cared for O Sensei at Iwama for many years, is now the caretaker and chief instructor of the Iwama *dojo*. He also works with Aikido Hombu Dojo for its continued preservation.

O Sensei died on 26 April 1969, and Aikido *dojo* around the world commonly hold special remembrances on that day to commemorate his life and his gift of Aikido. His way, his Aikido, is his gift of transcendence to anyone who comes to it.

It is interesting that O Sensei never took credit for being the source of Aikido. He said he was merely allowing the divine nature of the universe to move through him.

3 · THE PHILOSOPHY AND ETHICS OF AIKIDO

A mind to serve for the peace of all human beings in the world is needed in Aikido, and not the mind of one who wishes to be strong or who practises only to fell an opponent.

– Morihei Ueshiba

The basic philosophy of Aikido says that you not only have the right and the responsibility to protect yourself, but that you should also accept the responsibility to protect even those who transgress or attack you; that you should rise above any desires to destroy, and develop the ability to love all things.

Which would you say is better? Ten enemies before you, or ten friends behind you? To have ten that will back you up and pick you up, as opposed to knock you down and keep you down? Ten supporters – not detractors? So long as it does not compromise your own principles or negate your own or someone else's rights, it is far better to make a friend rather than an enemy whenever possible. This is the wisdom behind Aikido and I hope you will agree that this is a good way to go through life as well. We aspire not only to respect others, but also to develop the quality of character that communicates true concern for them.

While practising Aikido, that concern should be sincere enough that your partner, and even others around you, can sense it. They should feel it in their souls. Can they truly feel your concern or lack of it? They can – just as you can feel theirs. You are keenly aware of another's lack of concern because it affects you deeply; and the same will apply vice versa. Even if you are not concerned about what effect your actions may have on your partner, and the extended effect it has on others, you must realize that others will be aware of it. We are usually highly attuned to any threat to our well-being and safety, and because of this your partner may feel your lack of concern more acutely. Any casual, passive concern may not be apparent, and you must, therefore, extend yourself to transmit your genuine caring. This will better ensure that they get the message. Your challenge is to be absolutely sincere in your care and attention to others, and not to just act, or appear, that way. This is necessary for good Aikido.

The late Terry Dobson, a respected and progressive Aikido teacher and direct student of the founder, would go so far as to suggest that it is even your responsibility not to contribute to your attackers' *karma* by becoming their victim, and thus perpetuating their lot in life, their pattern of violence. But if you teach them a lesson in turn, with violence, ironically it serves only to strengthen their belief in its power. The balladeer, Nancy Griffith, also said 'If we poison our children with hatred then it's a hard life that we'll ever know'. We co-create our own reality.

Whether or not we acknowledge it, we are, to a larger degree than we realize, the authors of our own novels. We can create problems where none existed. We can fail to see the solutions that do exist. We can create solutions where before none existed. We can perpetuate our own pain and suffering. Or when we see that we do have the power of choice, we can, by a simple change in outlook or attitude, generate happiness and peace. What does it take to make this happen? It takes your decision to do so and your commitment to follow through.

The philosopher Goethe stated that the moment one commits oneself Providence moves too; that all sorts of things then occur to help one that otherwise would never have happened. When one decides to commit, doors that remained closed before – open. You gain direction for the energies that move through you and around you. You have listened to the voice of angels and they are eager to give their assistance.

With Aikido it is possible to turn enemies into friends by not retaliating in kind, by neither agreeing to nor allowing oneself to be their victim, by sincerely and genuinely caring for their well-being, making sure they feel and know you really care. You can defend yourself peacefully and non-violently without sacrificing yourself. You can even choose to protect the one who has attacked you from the energy and power of their own violence. With Aikido you can truly see them, feel them, understand them, accept them, take them in, change them instantly, and give a powerful gift of peace back to them by transforming them.

In Aikido technique the *aikidoka* enters into and deals with the deeper levels of the human psyche of the opponent. A connection is made to where that person truly lives. As an aikidoist you must be aware that most people, when confronted at deeper levels of their psyche, tend to be naturally more guarded, more suspicious, more nervous, and less trusting and accepting of others. Signals detecting insincerity in others can be loud and clear in the psyche. You may therefore have to work very hard at developing and transferring sincere caring for that person if you are going to make the healthy connection needed for your Aikido techniques to work properly. In order for them to accept, trust and agree to let you lead them, you must be fully present, and your sincerity must be genuine.

There are many corollaries of socio-ethical behaviour that can be drawn from self-defence training. Keep in mind that when you use violence or hatred to any extent, you encourage your opponents' revenge. In using hatred and violence how will your actions be perceived by those around you? Your behaviour could cause dissension, distrust, even anger and hatred among your own towards you. They may decide to attack you themselves because you could now be perceived as a threat to them. Now what do you do? Destroy, if you can, all those around you whom you love, who may even love you? You can see where this ludicrous example is going: nowhere productive. So, now that we have, hopefully, eliminated that choice let us move on to our other, more agreeable, options.

Here are some basic responses relating to self-defence:

1 Attack first before it appears you or others are about to be attacked. This may not be warranted and may be a gross over-reaction.
2 Defend yourself during the attack by retaliating with maximum destructive force. This, too, may not be warranted and a gross over-reaction.
3 Defend yourself by issuing back the same level of violence – 'an eye for an eye'.
4 Run away if possible. Abandoning your space may be okay but to abandon your family, for example, would not.
5 Negotiate: rationalize, plead, bargain that no harm will come.
6 Defend yourself effectively without causing any harm.
7 Perceive, evade and/or diffuse the situation before it closes in or escalates.
8 Defend yourself in such a way that you take care of the aggressor, even be responsible for their safety and forgive them for their loss of control and balance and help restore them to it.

Aikido enables one to have access to all these options. Its philosophy prefers, however, that the *aikidoka* elects the final scenarios. The *aikidoka* is learning and developing new ways of handling all conflict, not just those in the form of a physical attack. The strategies preferred in Aikido training make for effective, yet morally responsible living.

You may think that option 8 would be pretty hard to achieve, but this, however, would be exactly the desired response of an evolved master of benevolence and compassion. It is the ideal that all true aikidoists work towards. Difficult, maybe, but it may be easier to achieve than you expect. Let us put it in relative terms. Being an adult, you can forgive a small child for his or her actions, and you can understand and overlook a child's mistakes. Can you then forgive the child who has shown himself in the adult? We admire someone who is childlike. They show a simple, uncomplicated joy and wonder of life; they are able to openly share their peaceful core with everyone and everything. Yet we are all childlike. We are all children still, running around disguised in matured bodies. We all still pout when we don't get what we want. Inside we still want joy, seek wonder and desire peace, and we all still make mistakes. We can be unaware of the full repercussions of our actions. We can all feel regret and remorse over the outcome of our errors. These are further pieces of our shared reality. If you remember that, it will go a long way to soothing your intolerance not only of others but also of yourself.

There are always alternatives. You can deal in possibilities or impossibilities. Whichever you choose, positive or negative, your perceptions, your vision, your actions and the quality of your life will be tainted likewise from that moment on. Listen to your inner voice. It will guide you in your Aikido practice and your life. It speaks simply – yes or no. It may require a leap of faith and courage to trust in it. But listen to that voice and heed its counsel. Much of the time the most difficult thing to do is to break out of where you seem to be stuck and to try another tack – the reward may surprise you. Robert Frost wrote, 'two roads diverged in a wood and I – I took the one less traveled by – and that has made all the difference'. Listen to the wisdom of your deep inner voice and take a chance. When you learn to operate from the guidance of inner direction the deeper your grasp of Aikido will become. You will maintain your own balance, and be more in sync with everyone and everything around you.

Because Aikido is a tangible, physical way of learning about our common nature and encourages peace as the outcome, it is practised enthusiastically worldwide by people of all religions and all walks of life. Seeing ourselves in others, and acting accordingly, is a counselling common to religion, sociology, psychology and even responsible politics. In Buddhism, for example, one bows to another with hands pressed together in front of the face and body in a gesture called *gasho*. This is similar to the way the hands are held when praying in Christian practices. It is a gesture that means 'I recognize the God in you and it is the God in me'. Other religions may put it a similar way: that we are all 'children of God' or 'everything has Buddha nature' or that 'Jesus is within each of us' or 'the Great Spirit moves through all the creatures of the earth'. Aikido agrees with all these views; that we should all respect and love one another and the world around us. Aikido considers this not merely a concept but a reality, and if you desire to achieve its full benefits and maximize your understanding and proficiency of its techniques, it is highly recommended that you consider this basic premise. In true Aikido there can be no separation between this reality of commonality and interconnectedness and the reality of Aikido's techniques.

Once you can recognize that your practice partner is more like you than not, it becomes much easier to blend with their energy and their spirit. We see not an adversary but a friend or, at the very least, a potential one. The practice then becomes a joy, and this is when we realize that we are not so far away from our childhood as we thought. Being able to play opens up our learning valves; just as knowledge flowed into us unimpeded as children, we now allow ourselves to pulsate with the wonder of new discoveries.

We may not agree, but we can accept and understand a different opinion, a different belief, a different reality. We have not lived someone else's life. We have not been raised in their culture, been exposed to the nuances of their own personal world or experienced the same triumphs and traumas. But communication has to begin with one person. That person is sometimes the more courageous one.

In Aikido you must have the courage to begin that communication. You must develop the security and strength of character to be open; if you are not, how will you receive communication? Aikido enables you to engage life without losing the connection to yourself; to speak your mind without losing it; to act nobly without hesitation.

By showing us our common nature, a method such as Aikido can break down barriers to acceptance, communication and love. It can reveal why a rich man can be devastatingly poor, whereas a poor man can actually be abundantly wealthy. It can help us to understand what true prosperity is and what our role is in either destroying it or creating it. Seeing and feeling someone else's condition – their fear, anxiety, elation, pain, hurt, joy, frustration – can be an important insight. We can learn, on the mat and through our Aikido practice, that we, too, have the same range of experience and emotion. We can better see how others see us, and we can possibly even truly see ourselves.

As with any issue, awareness and recognition of a problem is the first step to solving it. Likewise, being aware of the options for behaviour that we all possess is the first stage in being able to then choose other, possibly more evolved, alternatives. Just as many studies have shown that given the right circumstances we all will kill. So it is that anyone, given the right circumstances, can evolve, can learn compassion, can choose life.

You have the moment-to-moment ability to choose and change your behaviour pattern. You always have options.

You can actively destroy
You can contribute nothing at all to yourself or the whole
You can take care of yourself and not others
You can take care of others and not yourself
You can take care of yourself and others

You have the power of choice. Choose wisely.

4 · CENTERING AND KI

Winning means winning over the mind of discord in yourself. It is to accomplish your bestowed mission. This is not mere theory. You practise it. Then you will accept the great power of oneness with Nature.

— Morihei Ueshiba

BEING CENTERED

What does it mean to be centered? Being centered means that one is in good balance on all levels – physically, mentally, emotionally and spiritually – possessing clear insight internally and externally, and capable of responding effectively to any stimuli. It means that you are in control of yourself. If you can control yourself you can better control the situations in which you find yourself.

How does one become centered? Two basic prerequisites are good posture and natural breathing.

It is easiest to find a centered state, or 'find your center', while standing, or sitting upright. From a physical standpoint your center is your body's physical center of gravity, located in the lower abdomen. The Japanese term for this area is *hara*, which is your spiritual center as well. This is where your gut, literally, speaks to you. You move from there, you feel from there, you sense from there. Aikido spontaneously springs forth from here.

There is a single point within the *hara* that is given more specific reference and attention: the *tanden*, or 'one point'. This point is approximately 2in below your navel. All Aikido movements work to emanate and flourish from this point – this center. It is from your center that your energy springs forth in all directions.

The challenge comes when you first take that centring into walking, then into other active movement and finally into high-intensity, high-stress activities. Aikido practice involves a wide range of paces and interactions in which to practise maintaining a centered state, everything from slow, controlled movements to the frenzied speed of, say, a multiple attack. If you can keep your center during these practices then it is a good indicator to remind you to maintain your center in your everyday life. Gaining knowledge and confidence on the mat enables you to keep your center during the stressful times in your life.

In Aikido, hopefully, we begin each technique being centered. Then this other person, our practice partner, comes into our space and affects our centeredness. Our natural reactions to this are varied. We may want to move in to meet them out of aggression, or move away out of uneasiness, or lock up out of fear – the fight, flight or freeze responses. Any of these can make us lose our center even if our body has not moved; if our mind is intimidated then we have lost our center.

This state of centeredness in meditation can be referred to as *fudoshin*, or immovable mind: 'mind that sits like a mountain'. Along with this concept comes *mushin*, or empty mind. This means to having an open, receptive, expanded state of mind that can move both itself and the body effortlessly in appropriate response to any stimulation. A centered state that combines both *fudoshin* and *mushin* presents no openings without awareness of them. *Suki* are openings or holes in someone's awareness or defences where an attacker can take the opportunity to launch an attack. The presence emitted by one who is centered, and whose *zanshin* is complete, gives no such openings. However, from a martial strategy sense, you can consciously create *suki* to draw the opponent's attention – to draw their mind. It then allows you to draw the attack in, giving you an immediate recognition of the attacker's intent. You are controlling the attack. You *know* before it *is*. You create the opening. They see it. They have the intention. They act on their intention. If your awareness is such that you created the opening in the first place, then you were in control the entire time. You were able to watch the whole process unfold. This is how you begin to learn to lead the attacker's mind. When feeling your partner's mind move into the opening you gain an important insight. The mind moves before the body.

Before you begin your move you have already envisaged yourself doing so. This applies to your attacker's mind as well. First comes the recognition that there is an opening for his attack. His mind has now already moved into the opening. If he feels confident that the attack will be successful then the body can be instantaneously launched into the necessary committed action. His *ki* then precedes him, and you can learn to sense and lead his *ki*; you can create openings or close them if necessary. If you allow no openings your opponent's mind will be evasive; it will jump around, looking for openings, evaluating strategies. By creating the opening, you can, without being obvious, be in control of the situation, his thoughts and his actions. In Aikido practice you can play and experiment with all of these factors.

Of course, an attack does not have to wait for an opening. Vigilance and *zanshin* are not necessarily guarantees against attack, but a centered state should not suffer for the surprise, suddenness or ferocity of it. If you are aware of your personal emanation of *ki* then you can more easily detect disturbances in its field, whether they originate from within or without.

POSTURE

Stand up, and try to stand still. Try as you might there is no way for you to be absolutely still. Take notice of the soles of your feet. There is constant adjustment going on; your body is constantly correcting itself. Feel how your weight is continually and subtly transferred to your toes, along the edges of one foot, to the heel of the other, to the balls of your feet, through your knees, and so on. This is your body seeking to maintain its balance – a comfortably erect posture. Evolution has given us the ability to maintain a standing position, from which we can see danger, move and survive it, and make use of our hands at the same time.

No matter how still your body may be, you must breathe. Your breath ebbs and flows, your energy ebbs and flows, your awareness ebbs and flows, your *ki* ebbs and flows. Your mind is perpetually active, expanding and receding, checking conditions around and within you. It is always dynamic, and it is the same for everyone else on the planet.

The link between body and state of mind can be most evident when examining posture. You can easily pick out someone who may be depressed or unhappy even by the subtlest of posture signals. And you can just as easily pick out those in a better frame of mind. You know when someone is agitated, angry, happy or drunk.

Being aware of your posture and changing it if necessary can have an immediate effect on your state of mind. That effect can be positive or negative; it is up to you. If you are not aware of your body or state of mind, however, you won't even know you have the choice. It was once said, 'Pain is a thing of the mind – and the mind can be controlled'. So it is that posture, and the pain, fear, arrogance and unresponsiveness that it can cause, can be controlled.

A body that is tense is experiencing stress. The tension created by stress keeps the breathing shallow, even laboured. The subtle nuances the body uses to maintain an efficient, relaxed posture are inhibited. The body is pulled subtly out of its preferred natural alignment. Muscles that could have remained passive are now called upon to keep the body rigid and erect. This creates an armouring effect on the body that is extremely undesirable for both effective Aikido and effective living.

This shielding, created by tense muscles, may give a certain feeling of security for some against the intrusion of a cruel world. However, it can also reinforce a state of denial – denial

29

of the signals that warn us of the dangers that appear regularly in many forms, some more threatening than others. Denial can get you into a great deal of trouble, particularly from a self-defence standpoint. For example: 'This street may seem unsafe but I'm not afraid – nothing will happen to *me* walking down it', or as General George Armstrong Custer said an hour before his death on a hill overlooking the Little Big Horn river, 'C'mon boys! We've got them right where we want them.' Denial can mean death – physically and also spiritually.

Both fear and arrogance can create and rule a body that is not open. It is likely that one encumbered with such a body will be able less able to respond appropriately and competently to life's challenges or a physical attack. Input received by a relaxed body may not get through a tense body. Valuable information that could allow natural instincts and intuition to flow properly and unimpeded is not received. A matter of life and death could end in the latter without this input. Judgement is affected. Reaction time is affected. Responsiveness is affected. Enjoyment of life is affected. A relaxed and comfortably glowing posture is open. With the absence of tension the body is able to make adjustments more naturally and with greater speed and efficiency.

Try this little experiment. While sitting where you are right now, take notice of your posture. As you brought your attention to it you may have even adjusted slightly to improve your posture. You may have instinctively lifted your head, sat up more erect, straightened your spine, even tilted your pelvis forward. In addition, at my suggestion that you take notice of your posture, your awareness kicked in. That awareness continues to be enhanced to an even higher degree with good posture.

Now bring yourself into a comfortably erect sitting posture. Do not rely on leaning against the back of the seat. Let your carriage align so that your weight settles through your pelvic bones. Elongate your neck gently and let your head float on it. Did you find your eyes looking left then right, or your peripheral vision becoming more alive? Your head even turning left then right? That is your natural awareness programming going into action simply because you brought yourself into comfortable posture. Now your mind and body are awake and ready. All your antennae are up and receiving. The body has evolved with this preference for proper posture for good reason: it allows for our natural survival instincts to go on full alert. The body can perform at its maximum abilities and speed. If you like, try the same awareness experiment while standing, then walking. Experiment with different postures and states of mind and even different emotions and see what each does, or does not do, for your being centered. Make a mental note of what contributes to a centered feeling and what detracts from being centered.

In Aikido we seek to maintain this naturally centered, comfortable posture. Good posture allows us to be more centered. It is, in truth, the primary reason we practise Aikido. A centered state is a peaceful state. Ideally, we should acquire this naturally balanced carriage before engaging with our practice partners. We desire to maintain the centeredness it brings throughout the performance of the Aikido technique as well as throughout our attacks and *ukemi* (falling ability). Hopefully, the byproduct of this training is a centered state we can take with us into the rest of our life.

BREATHING

Breathing is one thing you have in common with everyone else living in the world today, and it's obvious that breathing – for you, for me, for everyone – is pretty important. How important? Well, exhale fully and completely right now. Now do not inhale for as long as you can. You'll find that you have to take a breath pretty soon. Although you can do without food for maybe a couple of weeks, or without water for a couple of days, you can cope without breath for only a couple of minutes. I put it to you that you did not take a breath just now – you were given it. By what power is for you to ponder. You may have taken it – but it was given freely. Be thankful for the gift of life that your breathing brings to you in every moment.

Now that you appreciate the power of your breath to vitalize and restore you, you can better facilitate that power by first coming into a natural, comfortably erect posture. Once you do

31

this you may find your breath effortlessly expanding. You may even give out a slight sigh on exhalation. With the body erect and aligned, the shoulders can relax and flow to the sides, enabling the lungs to expand and the diaphragm to move freely. Tension dissipates; muscles relax; blood flows freely. With good posture, and the natural breathing that comes with it, you are now ready for Aikido training – or anything else, for that matter.

Aikido training gives special attention to the breath through various breathing exercises that are, more often than not, included in the warm-up exercises for class. Emphasis is given to the integration of the power of the breath into all Aikido technique. The breathing forms in Aikido may vary quite a bit depending upon a particular teacher's prerogative, but what they all have in common is the attention they bring to the breath, controlling it in order to both appreciate it and use it properly. As the breath is inhaled we draw in *ki*. *Ki* is drawn up from the earth and down from the heavens. It is gathered and settled into the *hara*; the meeting place of heaven and earth. We walk on the earth and in heaven simultaneously. Attention to breathing allows us to see that reality and give appreciation for it.

There is a particular basic Aikido technique called *kokyunage*, literally 'breath throw'. In fact, every Aikido technique could be called a breath technique because every one requires the integral use of proper breathing. Since your body and mind are practising the Aikido technique, and since both rely on the breath to function, the power of the breath must be allowed in and co-ordinated with the technique. Hence, one of the most important basic elements of Aikido is to develop *kokyu* power – breath power, or the power of the breath.

Observation of the breath in martial arts is very important. An attack is often initiated as the opponent inhales, and this inhalation is looked upon as an opening. While inhaling, the body is thought to be at a disadvantage. It is considered a moment of weakness, and so martial artists study to conceal their breathing, and its pattern, from an adversary. In Aikido, ultimately this does not matter. We can maintain a comfortable deep breathing that does not weaken our energy output or compromise our ability to respond. As the attack comes in we can breathe it in. We can welcome it, draw it in deeply, and dissipate it with our natural exhalation. We can take the energy of the attack and mix it with the energy we are inhaling. In this way we can draw the entire attack off its center and into our own. The energy of the attack is then ours; we control it and direct it from that point on.

In a typical Aikido breathing form the inhalation is done through the nose. The breath is then 'settled' to the lower abdomen, to the *hara* or the center. It is held there momentarily, then exhaled through the mouth. Inhalation and exhalation can be slow and sustained, or vigorous and explosive, depending upon the particular teacher's choice of focus. Whether doing breathing forms or simply focusing on your breathing, take notice of the pauses that precede or follow inhalation and exhalation. The cycle of each breath is a metaphor of the gift of life. Each reminds us of our own birth, existence and departure. Each comes from the great mystery that brought us and returns in the same way we will return. While drawing in the breath appreciate the fullness of the life it brings you. Then notice its waning. Notice its expiration. As you complete the exhalation, appreciate what the breath has given you. This pause is a mini-death. Take notice of it; for all of us there will be one last final completion of an exhalation – our last breath. Upon realizing that, you may now have an even greater appreciation for that next inhalation to come. It brings with it each time new life for you. Is it a gift? That is for you to decide.

Responsible Aikido training and this basic, profound appreciation for the life we all share are inseparable. It is a vital part of our common essence. The recognition and appreciation of such should work to complete us and bring us closer together.

GROUNDING

Now that you have learned about the power of your breath here is a typical Aikido exercise for learning about the power of your mind.

Stand naturally, feet comfortably apart. Have a friend gently push with their fingertips against your upper chest. As they do, you will eventually lose your balance and have to take a sudden step back to catch yourself.

Essentially what happened was that you lost your center, as a result of your attention being drawn to where your friend's fingertips were resting. Once your mind moved up, your center moved up as well and, as we all know, it is much easier to topple over something that is top-heavy. The full weight of your mind rising, and bringing your center up, enabled your friend to upset your balance. Conversely, the calm resolution of your mind settling roots you physically and energetically with the fullness of eternal presence. Letting your mind settle gives you back your center.

Try this experiment once again and this time, as your friend gently pushes, take the feeling of that push and allow it to go down to your center. It should require a noticeable increase in effort for your friend to move you. As you maintain your center and this pushing increases you will be able to step and move appropriately, without losing your equilibrium. The step back is not sudden and it does not relinquish to panic. A step back while maintaining your center is smooth and calm. It is grounded, yet floats effortlessly.

So, you have just learned a simple tool for centring but, more importantly, you have also learned how your mind controls the flow of your life energy – your *ki*. Your mind is much more powerful than you suspect. You have the power to direct your mind and your energy to where they benefit you best. Where you choose to put your mind can and will make a difference. Your mind is not limited to your head; it can go anywhere.

KI – THE PULSE & FLOW OF LIFE

Asian scholars, philosophers and theologians have had their varied and expansive definitions for the concept of what the Japanese refer to as *ki* for centuries. The recognition of what is called *ki* is not limited to Japan however. *Ki* can be defined as life energy, or life force; it can be called many things. Every part of the globe has its own words and definitions that try to define this something that is, essentially and ultimately, undefinable. The Chinese word, for instance, would be *chi* or *qi*. In India they may call it *prana*. Ask a Native American and the answer may be to call it 'the spirit that runs through all things'.

Everything has *ki*. Everything has a life force – an energy that runs through it and in it. It can flow or not flow, although even if we cannot perceive it, *ki* is always flowing. The rush of adrenaline may be explained as an extreme gathering of positive *ki*. Dogs can sense it. Predators of all species are probably very attuned to it. It is closely tied in with one's life force.

Quantum physics is now showing us that, indeed, at an atomic level, there is no difference between us and the trees and rocks that surround us. Everything consists of vibrating particles with immense expanses of space in between them. For our purposes of explaining Aikido the energy or life force that pulsates through all things can, therefore, be called *ki*. Aikido, again, means the way of harmonizing with this life force.

You have *ki*, right now, as a part of this living, breathing world. The very fact that you are breathing means that you are vital with *ki*. Proper breathing is the conduit for the flow of *ki*. Aikido's emphasis on *ki* and *ki* development exercises are actually *ki* recognition opportunities. The more aware you are of your personal flow of *ki*, the more you can affect its quality, cultivate it and embody it. Dicovering that you can affect the *ki* running through you enables you to use it properly, efficiently and more effectively. This recognition of one's personal flow of *ki* begins with attention being given to one's breathing, posture and quality of spirit.

The way we experience anything varies from individual to individual. So it follows that the way we experience and define *ki* will vary. One person's, or one culture's, attempt at definition should not be elevated, nor should it negate others.

Descriptions of *ki* range from simple 'energy' to 'the lifeblood of the universe', to 'the manifestation of the unification of *yin* and *yang*', to name a few.

There is a big difference between intellectualizing about *ki* and knowing it through the recognition that comes from being active and vital in its flow. It is the difference between listening to someone trying to describe the Grand Canyon and actually being there, surrounded by its awesome grandeur. How can you possibly adequately describe an experience you have had in a particular place to someone else who has never been there? They may get a semblance of it, but no matter how much you try they will not get your experience. So it is with *ki*. It *must* be experienced.

One thing is inevitable: that as you train in Aikido you experience *ki*. Intellectualization is not necessary for true understanding and true knowing. After the experience of body, mind, breath and spirit joining together in your Aikido training you can attempt to define your insights, but in trying to do so you may understand the definition's limitations. Keeping this is mind, I will, as a gift to you, attempt a humble description.

Ki is the life energy of creation that flows through all things in the universe. It manifests itself differently according to the form it takes and what existence it runs through. For you and me its flow is affected by factors such as vitality, age, health, attitude, perception, physique and life experience. It manifests itself differently according to subtle co-ordination of breath, body and mind. Where does *ki* come from? It is up to you to speculate.

Ki can be described as both positive *ki* and negative *ki*. In Aikido practice you can tell if someone's *ki* is flowing or not, if it is positive or negative, and how it affects their body, state of mind, awareness and performance. Aikido training typically begins with literal hands-on attacks or grabs. For instance, when taking hold of your partner's wrist, it is evident whether his *ki* is flowing outward or not. You can sense his spirit as well because the flow of his energy, his *ki*, is the signature of that spirit. The more presence, the more evident the flow, quality and vitality of his or her *ki*. This is a way to truly experience and know *ki* – to work with it in a real physical sense.

The first time I saw a demonstration of *ki*, and the power that was possible when the mind's direction was consciously controlled, was with the respected Aikido teacher, Koichi Tohei Sensei. He requested that two large men volunteer to hold each of his arms and pick him up while he resisted 'physically', as he described it. They picked him up without difficulty. Then, he said, he would resist them with his 'mind'. They tried to pick him up but could not budge him. I was amazed. I thought that the power of Aikido must be available only to superhuman martial arts masters, wizards and mystical monks. I discovered later, when I came to Aikido, that this feat can actually be accomplished by anyone. I found out that they could not pick him up because his *ki* and his mind connected him to the earth (*see* grounding exercise on pages 33–4).

It was not so much that he resisted their efforts. He recognized and accepted them. He simply did not allow them to pick him up. How is this possible? Have you ever tried to pick up a two-year-old who did not want to be picked up? Or move someone who is unconscious? Their weight is a 'dead' weight, and they can be much more difficult to lift because their mind does not agree with the action. It does not get caught up in the process and remains, either obstinately or unconsciously, where it is. If someone agrees to the lifting there is a lightness to them. Dancers know the power of this fact very well, and use it to assist their dance partner's lifts.

This grounding exercise has become a common Aikido demonstration that clearly shows the power of one's mind and how and where it can direct the natural power of one's *ki*. Anyone can do this. It does not require a black belt in Aikido, or mysterious superhuman abilities. At public demonstrations we call out people from the audience and they do it regardless of their physical size. It simply takes a bit of verbal guidance and suggested imagery.

Another typical Aikido-related demonstration of *ki* flow is called 'unbendable arm'. In this exercise your partner faces you and attempts to bend your outstretched arm as it rests on

Figure 2   The struggle of force against force

your partner's shoulder. To see the different effects you can, first, resist by clenching your fist (figure 2). This will require some effort on your part and it will draw your attention, your mind, into the struggle of your partner's efforts to bend your arm. If your partner releases suddenly, giving up the effort, your arm may bounce up just as suddenly in reaction to the loss of pressure. It may be injured in the process and throw your entire body off balance. Physically resisting his attempts will require some strength, struggle and effort on your part.

However, when you simply open your hand and let your mind and *ki* flow outward through your open fingers (figure 3), accepting and redirecting those elbow-bending efforts, you can actually neutralize their efforts. You recognize and accept the effort to bend your elbow, but your mind does not remain trapped there. This method of handling this exercise allows for a centered state. There is no struggle or effort. Your mind and your *ki* flow out to infinity. When the bending effort is suddenly lifted you will notice there is little or no loss of composure.

In Aikido, we often refer to the word 'extension' to describe one's flow of *ki*. We refer to good extension – good *ki* flow, and

Figure 3   Force being accepted, rechannelled and redirected

vice versa. Teachers may say you must extend your *ki*. They may relate your extension to the quality of your spirit or presence because your state of mind is so closely linked to the quality of your *ki* and, consequently, your extension.

While developing a strong extension do not lose your center. In Aikido practice the flow of your *ki* can be so overwhelming at times that you can lose your own balance and presence. Your own attention, your own mind, can be drawn off. You can be overextended. Overextension can be a physical sign of getting caught up in and drawn off by the strong flow of your own *ki*, and if this happens the power of your *ki* is greatly reduced. Certainly the only way to experience your limits is by reaching them. By reaching them we learn how to stretch them. We sometimes think that, as a friend of mine likes to quote, 'anything worth doing is worth overdoing'. This is a humorous reminder that the age-old wisdom of temperance and moderation in all things is good advice on the Aikido mat as well. You can miss a great deal because of overexuberance.

Poor extension and overextension are good indicators that more practice and presence is required. They remind us there is a balance between them. Good extension takes the middle road. Like words that have conviction, good extension must be rooted in presence.

Negative *ki* can be thought of as a sort of 'dark side of the force'. On the whole, people prefer to avoid those with negative *ki*. They may describe it as perceiving the person has a bad attitude. Others are intrigued by it and drawn to what seems to be its powerful effect. Most of us, however, if given the choice, would rather be in the company of those who exude positive *ki*. We may describe such people as being happier, as perhaps more balanced, possessing, conversely, a good attitude.

Whether you put out negative or positive *ki*, it will definitely have an effect on others. It is a fact of nature and of your existence; your *ki*, your energy, your attitude and how people perceive it are undeniable facts of life. It all becomes dramatically palpable on the Aikido mat.

When one comes to Aikido, *ki* development begins immediately. From the moment you are encouraged to open your fingers, such as in *tegatana* or 'sword hand', a hand posture common to a great deal of Aikido movement, you begin to feel its rush. O Sensei said, 'Spread your fingertips and let your *ki* flow to the ends of the universe.'

The responsibilities of having positive *ki* are to set a good example of attitude, energy and optimism; bringing it into all situations; and to make it available to those in need of it. Those who exude positive *ki* possess sincere, true, deep confidence and assertiveness. If your *ki* is weak you may be uneasy, and this can lead to many other problems. You may be much more vulnerable to afflictions from either outside or inside sources. It is the literal root of 'dis-ease'. Many will say that disease begins in the mind and, to a large extent, this is true since studies in science, medicine and other fields have proved that our attitude can have a profound effect on many circumstances and outcomes. If you do not already embody it, then positive *ki* development may require your cognizant attention. Easy does it. Bit by bit, step by step, day by day, moment to moment.

In the case of most people, like attracts like. Generally speaking, we choose to associate with those with whom we have more in common. We seek people to whom we can relate. Positive people tend to attract positive people, negative people tend to draw negative people. Be aware of what you are putting out. Positive *ki*, if too strong, can cause another's internal shields to go up. A steady, easy flow will allow their trust to come out. While practising Aikido connect to the person beyond the *ki* flow and beyond the mind behind it. Connect to his heart, his source. It is there that you can affect him and, hence, affect his mind and the flow of his energy.

Perception and point of view can also determine how someone will discern whether there is positive or negative energy. On the grand scale, nature and the workings of the universe do not attach good and evil aspects to positive or negative. They simply are. One cannot exist without the other. Their existence creates everything we see around us. Everything has its opposite. It is neither good nor bad; it simply is. There are just the *yin* and *yang*; each element has its opposite and everything just is. It is the *tao*. The indescribable. We are the ones who attach the values to what we see, feel and experience. We slant things according to our individual and collective perceptions. And we often cannot agree on those perceptions – who is right and who is wrong. Disagreements, disputes and wars are the result. When we can bring ourselves to accept and understand other perceptions, and realize that they are as justified as our own valid ways of perceiving, we then have the potential to dissipate conflict.

5 · THE LOOK OF AIKIDO

To compete in techniques, winning and losing, is not true budo. True budo knows no defeat. 'Never defeated' means 'never fighting'.

– Morihei Ueshiba

The practice of Aikido requires a minimum of several things: a qualified teacher, practice partners and, most importantly, a proper attitude. It helps to research Aikido and its philosophical aspects. On the whole, those who are already drawn to Aikido because of its ideology have the best foundation with which to begin studying the art. The philosophy of Aikido and the practice of its martial techniques are inseparable. After all, it is this ideology that forms the basis of Aikido practice. Like any martial art, Aikido is not something to be entered into lightly. Those who come to Aikido should not only be familiar with the ideas and theories behind it, but be fully committed and focused in their training from the start. They should have watched a typical Aikido class in the school of their choosing to familiarize themselves with the activity. Any martial art training carries with it the potential for injury; so one must be awake and fully responsive in order to get the most out of one's time on the mat.

42

Stepping onto the mat for the very first time is a very courageous act. Not so much because of the fear of injury, but the willingness to commit to change and growth. Change, even if we know it is for our own good, can be scary. It takes guts to put yourself in a position of vulnerability, where you must give your trust to others as they work with you and teach you; to show, like many of us, that you do not know everything, and you are willing and open to learning from others.

You are responsible for your being on the mat. If you do take that first step – congratulations. You have overcome a common fear – the fear of the unknown. You have shown that you have a pioneer spirit. It is a demonstration of bravery, but you are not alone; everyone who is practising Aikido today started the same way.

One must then accept the responsibilities that go along with the decision to study Aikido. There is no hiding on the mat. You are the only one responsible for your being there and in your training uniform – your *dogi*. You must now show respect for both yourself and others if you are going to have a healthy, rewarding and enjoyable experience.

Unlike a team sport where responsibility of success or failure is shared, on the mat it is your effort, or lack of it, that will determine your bounty. As in life, so it is on the mat – you reap what you sow. The right teacher can point the way but it is you that must walk the path.

In the vast majority of Aikido *dojo* the atmosphere is one of co-operation and mutual learning and encouragement. People work together to learn the nuances of the Aikido techniques and to help each other better understand the principles and ideas within the practice. There are smiles and good-natured sharing; learning together and interacting with a true feeling of camaraderie. It is an atmosphere of friendship and common commitment.

THE AIKIDO DOJO

The word *dojo* means 'place of enlightenment' or 'place where the way is practised'.

43

The typical Aikido *dojo* requires a mat because of the falling and rolling involved. It also usually has a *kamiza*, or 'place where the spirit of the *dojo* sits', sometimes called the *tokonoma*, where the members focus their attention when beginning or ending class.

The *kamiza* usually contains a photo of O Sensei as a symbol of respect and appreciation. It may hold any number of other items, such as a calligraphy scroll, a shelf of some sort for a flower arrangement or other special items, or an Aikido weapons rack with *bokken* and *jo* – it varies from *dojo* to *dojo*. There are no set rules.

Additionally, a *dojo* would usually require enough room to practise safely, dressing rooms and a desk for conducting *dojo* business transactions. *Dojo* that incorporate Aikido weapons as part of their training routine usually have ceilings high enough to accommodate the overhead strikes common to that practice, as well as racks to neatly and conveniently store those weapons.

The most important aspect of the *dojo*, however, is its spirit. If the spirit of the *dojo* is rich, from the teacher through the students who gather there to train, then the surroundings are far less important.

A TYPICAL AIKIDO CLASS

If you are interested in Aikido you should treat yourself and watch a class. Much will be explained that can never be covered here. You will see people in white uniforms with black skirts swirling, twirling and even flying through the air; black and white, white and black, *yin* and *yang*, hard and soft, fast and slow, simple and complex, love and hate, life and death. Watching a typical Aikido class is a visual reminder of it all and how it all exists at the same moment.

A typical class begins with the teacher and students bowing together to the main focal point in the *dojo* – the *kamiza* – in a seated and kneeling position called *seiza*. They then bow to each other, rise, and begin to follow the teacher in a warm-up session that involves deep breathing exercises, stretching and basic movement.

At the finish of the warm-up, the teacher will call upon a student, usually a senior, to give a particular basic type of attack. The teacher will demonstrate a basic response to that attack and, upon finishing, allow the students to practise the same sequence. The students then pair up and begin practice, or *keiko*. They take turns initiating the basic attack and then practising the technique. Each person will play one role of 'attacker' (*uke*) or 'defender' (*nage*) four times, then take the other role four times. They also practise both right and left, alternating within those four times. In a typical training sequence, for example, partners would practise the technique on the right side, then on the left side, then right once more, then left again, and then switch roles.

As the students practise, the instructor walks around the mat observing and giving correction and a suggestion here and there. The instructor may stop the entire class at times to make a point for everyone's benefit, then let them return to practising together.

After a short time the instructor will stop the class, usually either by clapping hands or calling out, and move onto the next technique. It is common for an instructor to keep the same attack throughout that class and go through a series of responses to it, moving from one variation to another. At the end of the class, lasting typically one hour (some *dojo* have longer classes – one and a half or even two hours), the teacher will call out or clap to finish. Everyone then lines up and bows out as a group to show mutual respect and appreciation.

At the end of the class the students follow the instructor in bowing first together towards the *kamiza*. Then the instructor turns around and bows to the students, who return the bow to him. Traditionally, the students then remain sitting in *seiza* while the instructor stands, walks to the edge of the mat, gives a final bow to the *kamiza* and then exits the mat. The students are then free to bow to any and all practice partners they had during that class. They should do both because it is the etiquette required in Aikido and because it is simply good manners. It shows your appreciation for what was shared during class, whether it was good or not so, and is the proper closure for an Aikido training session.

BOWING

Despite the founder's deep, personal religious beliefs and practices, Aikido, and the bowing associated with it, has no connection to any particular religion; Aikido accommodates all religions and spiritual pursuits. Bowing is used as a universally recognized demonstration of respect and appreciation. In Aikido we bow to show that respect and appreciation for the space we have to practise in (the *dojo*), our Aikido partners, our teacher, the founder of Aikido, the art of Aikido itself and what it does for us.

A bow is performed upon entering or leaving the *dojo*, stepping onto or off of the mat, and to our teachers and practice partners while on the mat.

While on the mat, traditionally speaking, the student should most often bow to the teacher from *seiza*, whether the teacher is standing or not. The bow of a student to a teacher is usually deeper in both its physical performance and its show of appreciation and respect. This also touches on the *sempai/kohei*, senior/junior, relationships common to Japanese etiquette and custom. In Japanese society, *kohei* defer to *sempai* not only out of respect but sometimes simply out of class status.

The bow should always be performed with sincere humility and appreciation. A good bow shows true presence. It should reflect an awareness, both internally and externally, of oneself and of one's surroundings. It should be void of conceit, arrogance or disdain. It should be humble, but not falsely so. An enlightened teacher will always bow in this manner to anyone.

A good bow should demonstrate one's humility. We show humility because that state will best allow learning. It allows information in with sincere appreciation. Arrogance closes off the mind making it difficult to accept new input, especially if it involves acquiescing, adjusting or changing. The lessons one learns through arrogance are often learned the hard way. A bow out of arrogance or superiority is closed and creates separation. Awareness is stunted. Conversely, a proper bow is open and receptive. All separation dissolves. Awareness expands both outwardly and inwardly.

Presence is a necessary state to strive for while in the *dojo*. It enables us to learn fully and be safety-conscious in the performance of a potentially dangerous martial activity. A good bow epitomizes presence. A good bow demonstrates integrated physical, mental, emotional and spiritual balance. It is fully aware and alive. Even if done quickly, it is not rushed; if done slowly, it is not lethargic. Its mindful performance should help to develop a trusting, humble and appreciative nature.

In other martial arts, eye contact is maintained with the opponent throughout the bow to show readiness and to be on guard for an attack. In Aikido, though, our eyes come off our partners to show our trust, our humility and our sincere appreciation for their practice with us. Taking our eyes off our partners also allows for many other advantages. Not looking does not mean not seeing. Not looking does not mean being unaware. Quite the contrary. Because we are not looking at our partners we cannot be drawn in by the holding power of their eyes, which can be a very captivating, even debilitating, force. Our other senses are brought into play, to bloom and open up so that we can sense and know what is going on without having to look. These senses include our sixth sense – the psychic sense – and its helpers, intuition and instinct. With our eyes off the other person we can begin to see with our mind's eye: to perceive that which the eyes cannot see.

When bowing as we enter or leave the *dojo* we show our thanks and respect for the physical and spiritual space we practise in. This is done in recognition of what the art of Aikido does for our lives and that of others. We show respect for ourselves and we acknowledge that coming to the *dojo* is a gift of love to ourselves, helping us to improve on all levels.

When bowing to our Aikido seniors, our *sempai*, those of higher rank than ourselves or those who have been practising Aikido longer than we have, we acknowledge the time they have put in and the efforts they have made to achieve their current level of Aikido understanding and proficiency.

With our bow we thank them for their presence. Some we thank for showing us how to perform better. Some we thank for showing us how we should do things. We may bow to thank others for showing us how not to do things. In other words, some seniors are good examples, while others, perhaps, are not – just like people you interact with every day. We should be thankful for both. We should learn to see ourselves in both and admit that we, too, can be seen as both a good example and a bad example. In our Aikido practice we can acknowledge this insight with one simple bow.

When bowing to juniors, our *kohei*, we must remember our own struggles, our own perception of how we viewed seniors. We should remember how intimidating new endeavours and sometimes new 'superiors' can be. We should bow humbly in appreciation of the depth of learning and insight the junior unknowingly brings to our own practice and understanding of the art that they do not feel themselves. Juniors teach seniors a great deal about the necessity of connecting to the other person. Seniors must be present with them in order to perform good Aikido technique. The junior may not know how to 'play along', like a senior *uke* would. A senior's *ukemi*, or falling ability, can make you look like an Aikido grand master without you having to concentrate at all. A senior *uke* can throw himself whether you are involved in the performance of the technique or not. A junior, on the other hand, and especially a beginner, does not know the routine, how to follow, when to take the fall. They must be led through every stage. The senior, therefore, must make a conscious effort to be fully aware and connected to the junior in order for the junior to be able to follow the technique. The junior is a reminder for the senior to always seek the evasive 'beginner's mind' where there is no room for complacency or boasting, and plenty of room for wonder and growth.

If you are going to progress in Aikido you need the challenge of both beginners and juniors. Just as juniors learn from seniors, seniors learn so much by working with beginners and juniors. The best aikidoists know the value of this and open themselves to juniors and beginners and the gift they offer.

As you see, we all learn from each other regardless if we are the teacher, the senior, the junior or the beginner. We are all students and, conversely, we are, again, all teachers. When bowing, however, we should always bow as a student – first and foremost.

PRACTICE CLOTHING

For practising, the Aikido student wears an all-white practice uniform called a *gi*, *dogi* or *keiko gi* (practice uniform). It is loose fitting and usually made of strong 100 per cent cotton. It consists of a sturdy jacket over drawstring pants. It is held together by a white cotton belt, called an *obi*, that is wrapped around the waist twice and tied in a knot at one's center.

The *dogi* for Aikido is, on one level, simply the best, most sensible, most practicable and most reliable clothing to wear

Figure 4   The dogi

because it is both comfortable and durable. On a more profound level, being white, it signifies purity and cleanliness of heart, mind, spirit and body, qualities necessary for growth in Aikido or any noble pursuit. Practically speaking, because it is white, it also shows uncleanness easily and must be washed regularly to not only restore and respect the *dogi*, but to restore and respect the person who wears it – you! Just as each day brings new life and new opportunities for learning, putting on a fresh, clean, cared-for *dogi* is your boarding pass to the new experience that you will find in each Aikido class.

The uniformity that the *dogi* brings in the *dojo* is also a symbol of how much we are all alike. It represents our commonality and how we share so much: our struggles, our desires, the ground that supports us, the air that gives us life. We all experience hardships and triumphs. Life is a group experience and we go through it together. The *dogi* is the mirror that shows us that we, too, exist there: in others and outside of the *dogi* to which we think we are limited. It shows our integration; our common links. It demonstrates, in the *dojo*, our common commitment to bettering ourselves.

The belt or *obi* holds your *dogi* jacket in place, yet is a symbol of your personal commitment. As the knot is secured properly at your center it brings you into focus, ready for the training to come. The *obi* gives a further physical sense of your *hara*, where heaven and earth meet. The *hara* is your center of gravity, as well as your spiritual center, connecting you to your psyche and to the universe. Therefore, when the knot is tied, one is complete, internally and externally, and ready for Aikido practice.

Most Aikido *dojo* have a structured ranking system starting at white belt and progressing to black. A *dan* rank is a black-belt rank. *Shodan*, for instance, refers to first-degree black belt. The various ranks below black belt are called *kyu* ranks, and there are usually five of these. These *kyu* ranks usually wear only white belt until attaining black-belt level. However, some Aikido *dojo* and organizations use a coloured belt system to denote the level of *kyu* rank attained.

The pleated skirt-like garment worn in Aikido is called a *hakama* (figure 5). Its use accentuates the beauty and grace of

Aikido movements, *ukemi* and techniques. It is usually entirely black, but indigo or dark blue are common as well. It is generally worn by black-belt levels, but some *dojo* allow the students to wear them regardless of rank. For many years, and even today in some Aikido organizations and *dojo*, males could only wear the *hakama* after achieving black belt while women could wear it from the start. This system began because of Japanese customs of modesty. However, this can vary, and in my own *dojo* we have elected to eliminate what can be viewed as double standards, and allow all students at third *kyu* level to wear the *hakama*. This is about halfway to black belt, by which time they have been practising diligently for several years and are proficient enough to warrant it by traditional standards.

When one is given the privilege of wearing the *hakama* it can become an appreciated tool for new insights. Tying it properly and caring for it responsibly is mandatory for it to expand your experience of Aikido. The knot of the

Figure 5   The hakama

hakama should enhance the *obi*'s attention to the *hara*. The *koshita*, or lower back plate, should remind one of the importance of good posture which allows for good breathing, necessary for centering which, in turn, allows for maximum performance and learning. The full skirt of the *hakama* gives one a sense and palpable feel for the flow and grace of Aikido movement. You float and swirl through practice; you can feel your gracefulness. At the end of class the personal ritual of folding the *hakama* properly brings a closure to practice. It shows respect for the *hakama* and for the lessons learned while wearing it. It also offers a transition period for us into the outside world.

6 · THE PRACTICE OF AIKIDO

We ceaselessly pray that fights should not occur. For this reason we strictly prohibit matches in Aikido. Aikido's spirit is that of a loving attack and that of a peaceful reconciliation. In this aim we bind and unite the opponents with the will-power of love. By love we are able to purify others.

— Morihei Ueshiba

AIKIDO TRAINING

Aikido training consists of learning both to lead and follow a partner as a basic method of understanding the flow of the Aikido techniques. The basic practice requires a pair of students to work together taking turns being 'attacker' and 'defender'. As mentioned earlier, the attacker is referred to as *uke*, the one who receives the Aikido technique, and the defender as *nage,* who performs the Aikido technique.

For example, *uke* gives the specific attack being focused on and then follows *nage*'s lead in response to that attack. It then makes sense that if *nage* does not lead *uke* properly and effectively, *nage* will be unable to perform the Aikido technique properly and effectively. Likewise, if *uke* does not follow *nage*'s lead with heightened awareness and sensitivity, *uke* may be unable to blend with the Aikido technique that is being performed, and so be unable to absorb its power and survive safely. Since there is potential for injury to either person while practising Aikido techniques, it is imperative that both be fully aware and agree to watch out for the other's safety as well as their own.

Both must agree to trust the other when practising a particular technique. Each practice (and I emphasize, again, that this is practising only – not competing) requires a specific technique response to a specific technical attack. Please keep in mind that this is a training method necessary for the proper grasp and development of specific basic Aikido technique. This is *kihon waza*, or basic technique. As one becomes more accomplished and comfortable with Aikido technique, then one develops the ability to respond naturally and seamlessly to variations, elaboration and intensities of the attacks, all the while maintaining calm, unruffled control. This method of engaging the technique during its full movement is called *ki no nagare*, or flowing techniques. Still later, the techniques become freestyle responses called *jiyu waza*.

Aikido practice can be vigorous or cautious, but it should always have mutual safety and respect as its priorities. This is one of Aikido's most important traits, and enables anyone, regardless of gender, size or age, to experience its benefits. In fact, maturity of years only enhances one's Aikido. The option and the ability to use physical strength become less desirable. With maturity comes a greater understanding and recognition of our bodies and a deeper wisdom of the cycles, the rhythms, the ways of nature – of life.

Effective Aikido technique comes about when one moves in and with these principles of nature. The body learns these principles much faster and more fully than the intellect. What the body knows cannot be easily or adequately verbalized or explained by our intellect. When we are trying explain to someone else what we have learned through our body and spirit during Aikido practice it can be frustrating. It is not unlike giving someone a photo of a beautiful place we know well. One can get some idea of what that place is like, but in order to really experience it and know it in the same way you must experience it physically.

It is not uncommon for beginners, in the excitement of fresh discovery, to attempt to describe Aikido to others so that they can experience it too. When words and attempts at descriptions fail or appear inadequate, they may simply say, 'Well, here, let me show you – grab my wrist.' This is a common request, since wrist grabs are one of the best methods for teaching Aikido to beginners. Extreme caution should be taken when demonstrating your newly learned skills. In your desire to convince someone of Aikido's effectiveness you may catch them by surprise in your enthusiasm, and it is all too easy to injure someone by being insensitive, irresponsible and reckless.

Generally speaking, it is wiser to keep your knowledge quietly to yourself, especially in the case of people you don't know well. The need to show off new skills, whether out of enthusiasm or bragging, can be asking for more trouble than you can handle. This is known as 'white-belt syndrome' amongst martial artists and shows that a little knowledge can, indeed, be a dangerous thing. There are many detractors out there waiting to criticize and challenge. Letting a stranger know you study a martial art like Aikido can be like dropping the gauntlet, and may lead you into all kinds of unwanted trouble.

The more you study Aikido, or any of the martial arts, the more you know how dangerous a physical encounter can be for both yourself and someone else. An accomplished martial artist does not seek this, especially if they have true confidence. They prefer to keep their skills to themselves, out of both humbleness and wisdom. For those who are astute in the tactics of attack and defence, it is also a valid martial strategy not to reveal your full capabilities to a potential attacker lest they see your limitations and work out a way to take advantage of them.

One of the basic methods of teaching Aikido common to all Aikido *dojo*, as I mentioned, is from basic wrist-grabbing attacks, *Katate-tori*, where *uke* grabs *nage*'s wrist (figure 6). The attacker may intend to follow that grab with a punch or

Figure 6   Katate-tori

kick. These basic grabbing attacks teach the practitioners, quite literally, in a 'hands-on' way, about basic distances or *ma-ai*.

Ma-ai, meaning time/distance, is usually used to describe the distance between two partners. These various basic grabbing attacks offer many excellent insights. With these wrist grabs the attacker and the attack have come just inside your safety zone. The urges to flee, fight or freeze are triggered and accentuated by physical contact, and we can literally feel the attack and our partner's level of commitment to it and us. From this distance, up close and personal, natural instincts and reactions, both good and bad, come to the forefront. We don't have to think about calling them up, they simply take over. Feeling the various reactions of flee, fight or freeze, and their effect on our bodies, brings us an acute awareness of their effect on our ability to respond. We can then learn to override them or go with them as the case may be. We get the chance to trust the body's learning and knowing, while keeping intellect in check (*see* page 58).

Wrist grabs set up a distance that is important to work with and become comfortable with for many reasons. Tolerant or terrified, brave or fearful – all will allow a threat to come into their space to this extent. In most situations, especially in a physical attack, you have to deal with the person face to face, or even with your back to the attacker's face. Most conflict gets up close and personal. This distance is, therefore, one of the most basic and most valuable practices of Aikido.

When you grab your partner's wrist, you grab reality. A knowing is going on that requires no explanation. You know that there is another living, breathing person making contact with you. While training within this basic distance we are able to practise Aikido's almost limitless range of techniques and variations. Besides grabbing, *uke* is within striking and kicking range as well. Learning to be effective with this distance, and the variations of speed possible from it, gives us the knowledge, experience and confidence necessary to perform these same techniques as the attacks change: becoming much closer (grabs or strikes to the face, chest, abdomen, shoulder, throat and so on); or increasing in distance, speed and intensity; or even coming from other directions.

As experience and proficiency increase, Aikido practice expands to include weapons attacks, using such traditional weapons as the *bokken* and *jo*, as well as knife and multiple attacker scenarios. Practice will even include both partners performing techniques on their knees, called *suwari waza*, or with defender kneeling and attacker standing, called *hanmi handachi*. It is not as though in a real-life situation we may have to defend ourselves on our knees, but training in the techniques while on our knees teaches us to move our bodies from our centre and from our hips. If we can move easily on our knees through techniques and generate the power required for their effective execution, then that ability translates even more powerfully and more effectively into full standing techniques. In addition, with the case of *hanmi handachi*, you can learn a lot about how to move effectively when faced with larger, taller opponents and how to neutralize their attacks with confidence despite their apparent advantage of height and size.

Moving beyond static grabbing attacks to being attacked from a distance or in movement should, theoretically, be easier since you now have the luxury of more time and distance with which to respond. Or so we may believe. When the attack comes from a distance, or in movement, the challenge is to not let the intellect shut down instinctive movement. Now that there is time for the intellect to come into play, it will try to stop everything, to freeze it in an attempt to analyze the situation and suggest options. The body may know it should move, but the intellect may keep it from doing so by saying, 'Wait a minute! Let's think about this.' Big trouble will loom over you as a consequence of your hesitation. In real life-and-death situations, 'he who hesitates is lost', and, frankly, he who hesitates may very well be dead. When the intellect speaks up, the mind and body should be allowed to reply instantly with 'Well, you can think about it while we're on the move.' This acknowledges and properly uses all the attributes at our disposal.

This can sometimes cause new Aikido practitioners to pause. If they cannot intellectualize what their body and spirit are experiencing, they take on a puzzled look. Their intellect does not quite understand, and since society puts so much emphasis on intellect, the new practitioner can repress, override or even invalidate the very real learning that is going on.

Now don't misunderstand, having the intellect step in and say 'Wait a minute' can be a very good thing, especially for those who require the analysis factor to feel comfortable with what their body is experiencing and maybe already comprehending. This is absolutely necessary with the initial learning of a technique. In the context of basic static, or slow practice, where one can create and control time without dangerous results, minimal analysis will be quite helpful. Analyzing Aikido technique is fine, though one must remember that while the intellect may be able to describe what is going on, it is the body that knows it. Experience is the best teacher. True learning will take place so long as analysis remains within the proper context, and the intellect is allowed in by the mind/body/spirit as an additional tool for further understanding, guidance and growth. Its opinion should be considered as a piece of the whole, with the mind, body, spirit and intellect working together to commonly learn and grow together.

In Aikido, the intellect is used to help us better see, hear and further comprehend the instructor's guidance: where to put our feet, our hands, our bodies and our energy. It helps us to understand and explain what is going on in the technique – explain it and describe it – but it is the body and spirit that experiences it. The intellect knows of it, can give witness to it, and can describe it extremely well, perhaps, but it is the body that takes you there and actually shows you. The intellect can put the theory out, but it is the body that knows if it will work or not.

Non-verbal, body-to-body learning needs no translation. When a technique is practised body to body, one human being with another, the learning occurs naturally, directly and deeply. Your core experiences it. No explanation is necessary or adequate for that matter. So much information is downloaded once the physical connection is made that no deciphering is needed, no intellectualizing need be done. It is direct transferral. One receives it and knows it.

Again, this is not meant to negate our intellect. We must give thanks for the benefits we receive from this gift and welcome it no more or less than our other gifts. And we must use all of our gifts wisely.

As you probably know, science, a product and wonder of intellect, was originally repressed because it threatened our connection with the world and spirit behind it. Science was viewed as anti-spiritual; so, naturally, religions were antagonistic towards it. Science, after all, seeks and requires proof; religion requires faith. Now, ironically, science and spirituality are coming together. As I mentioned earlier, science is now showing us, through quantum physics, that we are, indeed, at a basic atomic and molecular level, not only all the same, but all connected and inseparable. This, as you know by now, is the basic premise of Aikido.

Our intellect, therefore, helps us to understand what is already a reality. The danger may be that we have learned to rely on and live in our intellect so much that we have separated ourselves from the balance of our body's knowledge, intuition and instinct. This is where our spirit truly lives and thrives; the intellect merely takes pictures. In the context of Aikido training our intellect should be a welcome companion that is integrated with the other aspects and attributes of our true nature, not an internal combatant that gets in the way of truth and real knowledge.

BLENDING

In Aikido, when one faces opponents, one must not see them as separate, for there truly is no separation. When our opponents move we are already moving because we have felt their minds move. Their attack is joined with openness and even welcomed. This allows for a spontaneity of movement to flow through us, naturally placing us out of the way of harm. This is the essence of *musubi*, or blending.

Once *nage* has blended with *uke*'s attack, *nage* draws the energy of the attack into his own centre, making *nage*'s centre the centre of the entire interaction. *Uke*'s balance has been compromised and is now controlled by *nage*. The energy and outcome of the attack is now also controlled by *nage* as well. *Nage* can then dissipate the attack's energy or add more to it for an explosive and dramatic climax.

A demonstration of Aikido by two advanced *aikidoka*, with an all-out attack and full response, would be something like this: as an attack is launched the *aikidoka* joins with it, becoming a powerful vortex. *Nage* is the whirling tornado as *uke* is snatched up in its expanding force. *Nage*'s centre is the calm eye of the hurricane; *nage*'s body movements the fury of the typhoon. Once released or launched *uke* is left bewildered and stunned as to how he came to be on the ground.

In order to blend effectively with our opponents we must open our heart to them and fully allow ourselves to feel their presence, their pain, their hearts. Then there is no guessing as to what their intent is and what actions will follow. Knowing this in advance, we can then maintain our compassion while not becoming the recipient of their off-balance actions – in other words, their attack. When one develops this depth of insight and can function from it, one can, from a *karmic* sense, play an important role in changing someone's life. When violence no longer has a victim to vent its energy upon, that energy remains with the one who fostered it. It does its damage there. And, of course, the one afflicted with this energy, this disease, wants to release it once again.

In Aikido you have the opportunity to see this scenario unfold. If you allow that energy to go harmlessly through you, you can then transform or replace it with your love and compassion, which for all of us is an amazingly powerful force. In changing someone's world for the better you change your world for the better too, and since there is only one world, you have actually simultaneously changed the world. Your simple act has not only changed reality, but it has given notice of such to the ends of the universe.

UKEMI – THE ART OF FALLING

Ukemi is the ability to receive the technique and fall away from the harm it can cause. In Aikido, being *uke* means that you give the attack, performing the necessary grabs and strikes. You then receive and absorb the Aikido technique, blending with it to take the fall and survive it properly and safely. This is called 'taking *ukemi*'. *Ukemi* is an important aspect of Aikido training. It is the other half of Aikido practice.

Ukemi requires one not only to be able to deliver the wide range of attacks, but also to be able to respond quickly and appropriately to the specific Aikido technique being practised by *nage*. Usually a specific Aikido technique, or its variations, requires a specific *ukemi* technique. There are basic techniques that are matched with basic *ukemi* as there are advanced techniques that require advanced levels of *ukemi*.

The ability to 'take *ukemi*' is a much admired and much sought-after skill. It means, on one level, that you are more likely to be called out by the instructor to assist in the

Figure 7   Aikido forward roll

demonstration of the Aikido technique. This is both an honour and a responsibility. When called up in front of the class
to take *ukemi* you must be focused on what the instructor
wants – what specific attack you are expected to perform, and
to what degree of commitment and intensity. You should
then show how to give the attack properly and demonstrate
the required *ukemi* in receiving the instructor's Aikido technique. The instructor is relying upon you to show the proper
ukemi – the other half of the Aikido practice.

It is hard to describe here, perhaps, but much is transferred
when taking *ukemi* from an instructor. As *uke* you are experiencing first hand the effects of the instructor's technique.
You are a privileged part of the instructor's gift – the instructor's technique itself. You receive this teaching directly. It is
'hands-on' learning in the truest sense.

In general, taking *ukemi* leads to a higher skill level of
one's ability as *nage*. Many think they are only learning
Aikido when they are in *nage*'s role, practising the Aikido

technique. However, *uke* is practising Aikido as well. The practice of coming in with the agenda of the attack, and having to give up that agenda in order to blend and adjust instantly and fluidly to the Aikido technique, translates exceptionally well into one's understanding and grasp of the principles and power of Aikido.

Proper *ukemi* requires *uke* to have a certain level of commitment in the attack to warrant a response from *nage*. That commitment can have various degrees of focus, speed, power and intensity depending upon *nage*'s level of ability to handle that practice. The attack can be tempered to accommodate beginners, for example, allowing them to examine the necessary body, hand and foot movements, or it can be a full-out, intense attack. The more strongly an attack is launched, the faster, the more severe and the more dangerous the responding technique can potentially be.

When *nage* is receiving a strong attack from *uke*, a higher level of Aikido skill may be needed on *nage*'s part to take a severe attack, control it, and calm it, instantly, completely and safely. As *uke*, you can easily set yourself up for injury if your *ukemi* skills are not up to the intensity level of your attack. As *uke*, you must keep your awareness keen and your movements sharp and responsive in order to feel *nage*'s lead as you are taken through the Aikido technique.

In *nage*'s role, if your *uke* does not feel connected to you, he or she cannot be led. *Uke* cannot 'feel' you, cannot 'hear' you when you suggest with your leading, 'I would like you to come this way'. You must blend with *uke* and provide the leadership and direction for *uke* to follow. Aikido requires finesse – not force.

Aikido is less about insistence. It is more of a polite suggestion – sometimes vigorous, sometimes gentle.

AIKIDO BASIC STANCES

The basic stance in Aikido is referred to as *hanmi* (figure 8). *Hanmi* means 'half body.' In this stance you face your opponent obliquely. There is right *hanmi*, or *migi hanmi*, and left *hanmi*, or *hidari hanmi*. When the hands are placed in front of the body while in this position the stance is then called *kamae* (figure 9).

After achieving a comfortable, centred standing posture, move your right foot forward maintaining a comfortable distance between your feet. By moving your right foot in front you have achieved, in this case, a right *hanmi*. This position should allow grounding yet not inhibit easy movement in any direction. The upper torso can comfortably face the front and, again, allow for effortless movement in any direction in relation to one's partner/opponent. Your knees are not locked or rigid but comfortably supple.

From this position raise the hands, keeping them relaxed. Take notice of the feeling they have. Now lower them again to your sides.

Now open your hands, splaying the fingers. Allow your energy to flow through your fingers and palms as you raise your hands to the same position as before. Take notice of the feeling in them now. Did you feel the difference once you simply opened your hands and allowed your energy to flow?

Figure 8   Basic hanmi *or stance*

Figure 9   Basic kamae *or ready stance*

This is a basic *kamae* which is sometimes called 'ready stance' or 'fighting stance'. Experiment with both exercises to observe the subtleties of your *ki* flow, grounding and overall awareness.

After feeling the effects of co-ordinating your mind, body and energy, you can move that same awareness of the flow of energy through your hands into other parts of the body such as the feet and top of the head. You may be able to perceive that there is a simultaneous flow of that energy both in and out. Know that your entire body both emanates and receives that energy – that is *ki*.

TAI NO HENKO

A basic partner exercise, common to most Aikido *dojo*, is called *tai no henko*, meaning body adjustment or body change. It is sometimes called *tenkan* exercise. *Tenkan* means to turn.

65

Figure 10   Nage *matching the flow of* uke*'s energy*

In this practice you offer your hand so your partner can grasp
your wrist with his opposite hand. His left grabs your right,
for instance. Once he grasps your wrist, allow your energy to
flow through your fingertips as in the previous exercises for
kamae. Your energy flows into him as his flows into you
while you maintain yourself and your centredness. You can
then match his energy flow by moving your hand in the
direction of his energy with your fingertips pointed back
towards you (figure 10). Maintaining the positive flow of
your energy, slide your front foot forward slightly and to the
near outside of your partner's lead foot. Turn your hips in the
same direction as their energy flow and your forward hand's
fingertips, again maintaining your centering. After achieving
this slight entry, and agreeing with your partner's energy
flow, draw your outside hip back. This will also draw that
same foot back into what is a mirror image of your partner's

66

hanmi. In other words, if he has his right foot forward, grabbing with his right hand, then you will now be in a left *hanmi.* Add both your hands in the same direction, with all your energy blending and flowing in the same direction as your partner's (figure 11).

There is actually a great deal more to it than can ever be fully explained here – including *uke's* role. That is why you need a qualified teacher. For instance, if you do not learn to connect with the partner who is grabbing you, you will not affect him as you move, essentially wasting your body movement. At the point where you are a mirror image of his *hanmi* you should have subtle control of his posture, balance, energy flow and centre. His effectiveness will be neutralized when this exercise is practised properly.

Once again, the only way to learn this exercise is through the guidance of a knowledgeable Aikido teacher. This simple exercise, is, in reality, so complex that you can perform it

Figure 11 Nage, *having blended entirely, moves safely to* uke's *side and is now in control of* uke's *energy, balance and direction.*

thousands of times and still learn from it. Each time you practise it, it is different; although not everyone has the insight to recognize it. I offer it here as a sample of a basic Aikido partner exercise that is almost exclusively and universally practised in Aikido *dojo* around the world. Keep in mind that this is a limited description, and that *tai no henko*, like most Aikido techniques, can be and is practised with a fascinating variety of emphasis and nuance.

AIKIDO WEAPONS – *AIKI-KEN* & *AIKI-JO*

Once experiencing and practising awareness and control of the flow of energy, you can take that, for instance, into the Aikido weapons practices called *aiki-ken* (figure 12) and *aiki-jo* (figure 13). In *aiki-ken* a *bokken* (wooden sword) is used; in *aiki-jo* a *jo* (wooden staff). Both are usually made from a hard wood such as white oak.

Figure 12   Aiki-ken

Most, but not all, Aikido *dojo* integrate or offer training in *bokken* and *jo*. Those teachers who do, consider the hand-to-hand and weapons training the same. Some do not stress regular weapons training, believing that what would be learned through the use of weapons can and should be learned through diligent hand-to-hand training. Many will point out that O Sensei himself used *aiki-ken* and *aiki-jo* to teach Aikido. In his later years, however, many of his direct students say that he would admonish them sternly if he found them practising with these weapons. He told them that it was a waste of time – that he had already done that work. Still, many want to explore Aikido's roots and experience first hand the transitional insights that weapons practice offers.

Let's look at how Aikido's weapons, *aiki-ken* and *aiki-jo*, can enhance our Aikido.

Aikido weapons are practice partners. They can teach us much and they can cause us and others injury if not

Figure 13   Aiki-jo

respected and properly used. Weapons training can do much to enhance one's grasp of Aikido's many aspects. One certainly learns about being calm, centred and responsive, while dealing with an enhanced level of fear, since one can be injured by someone else's practice weapon. Co-operation and safety are still adhered to in weapons practice so this isn't really a pressing concern. Weapons training brings new insights for mind expansion, use of the body, footwork, speed and intensity, energy flow and redirection. Training with these tools gives one a good understanding of distance and timing, and how it applies to effective Aikido technique. Specific footwork and body/hand movements can and do relate directly back to specific Aikido hand-to-hand techniques. Training with the *bokken* and *jo* allows one to move one's awareness and energy through and beyond one's physical limitations – an ability that is essential to good Aikido.

Bokken is usually considered a preliminary to *jo* practice. *Bokken* practice, in its basic form, is more structured and, therefore, is usually the first Aikido weapon to be recommended to a beginner. The hands, in its basic practice, can remain in relatively the same place on the *bokken* as in basic kamae. The *jo* is, fundamentally speaking, more fluid, creative, versatile and expansive. The hands can switch places using either end of the *jo*. As one's understanding of these two weapons practices increases, one realizes they actually have more similarities than differences.

Practice with *bokken* or *jo* can be solitary, which, in an art that mainly requires a partner, can be a useful adjunct to training. *Aiki-ken* and *aiki-jo* are one aspect of Aikido practice that can be done at home alone. The individual strikes, cuts and movements that can be practised alone with either the *bokken* or the *jo* are called *suburi* – specifically, *bokken suburi* and *jo suburi*. During *suburi* practise you concentrate on performing and perfecting basic strikes and body movements along with your *te no uchi*, or hand gripping, endeavouring to co-ordinate your energy, mind and body with those movements.

Suburi practice is especially necessary and helpful when one is initially being introduced to weapons training. This is also a useful practice when one does not have a practice partner. *Suburi* enables the student to work on subtleties of body movement at home, for instance. As the years go by the insights that can come from continued exploration of *aiki-ken* and *aiki-jo* never end and provide a rich source of new learning.

After familiarity with basic *suburi* we move on to partner practice. There are two-person *bokken* forms which are called *kumi tachi* and two-person *jo* forms which are called *kumi jo*. Both have a variety of simpler blending movements for two-person practices as well.

Some of these forms integrate, to larger or lesser degrees, *kiai*. *Kiai* is the unification of the spirit, body and voice coming through a penetrating scream that explodes out from the *hara*, one's centre. Many *aikidoka* incorporate this *kiai* with both their weapons training and with their regular training. This experimentation with the use of sound can be yet another vehicle for gathering and focusing one's individual and universal energy and spirit. It is another way of moving the breath and energy throughout and beyond the body.

Another weapon commonly used in Aikido practice is the knife or *tanto*. Training against the *tanto* teaches one about proper body positioning and movement as well as centering against such a quick and versatile weapon. *Tanto*, like *bokken* and *jo*, are made of wood, usually a hardwood, such as white oak or ash. It is usually a single-edged blade facsimile. Basic Aikido techniques can be practised against a wide variety of knife thrusts, stabs, strikes or slashing attacks. There are a few exceptions, but on the whole there are no *suburi* practised with the *tanto*. Only *tanto-tori*, or knife-disarming techniques, are practised. Practising Aikido techniques against weapons attacks sharpens our Aikido basics. For instance, a properly performed *tai no henko* will neutralize a thrusting stab attack (see *tai no henko*, page 65).

Whenever practising with Aikido weapons, remember that we are not merely doing weapons work. We are doing body work. We are learning more about how to use the body and its energy properly. We are further exploring *tai sabaki*, or body movement. We must not be distracted by the feeling of power that weapons work can offer. We are practising Aikido principles. If you think you are studying a valuable skill that will enable you to cut an enemy down with a sword, or whack them on the head with a staff, you are missing the point. Weapons work can fool many of us: we think we are learning to defend ourselves, but in reality how often do you walk down the street with your sword or staff? Or, for that matter, when was the last time someone attacked you in a car park swinging a 5ft wooden staff?

Working with Aikido weapons can further teach you about your own body and how to move energy through it effectively. It opens up your awareness, and makes you deal with the fear of getting struck while still maintaining center. It teaches you how to generate power, move it through you and extend it without losing your grounding or composure.

Defensive techniques against Aikido weapons again give us the opportunity to maintain our composure despite the apparent advantage of our opponent's weapon. Because our partner has an extended reach with these weapons, and because their use covers a wide range of angles of attack, we learn to move more fully and effectively when having to defend against them. These defensive techniques usually include disarming the attacker as well.

At its basic level, *bokken* and *jo* practice allow the opportunity to move your energy and awareness into that tool and then beyond it so that as you make contact with your practice partner, you instantly move your energy into them, and then through them when throwing. This should all be done while maintaining one's centerd state.

Weapons training also teaches us about the footwork, timing, distance and specific use of the body for very specific Aikido techniques that are related to specific weapons techniques. Many Aikido techniques can be compared to, and explained by and through, weapons techniques.

In fact, Aikido techniques have more in common with cutting than with grabbing; they extend and cut rather than grab and pull. Any grabbing is applied with the same extended flow of *ki*. If you merely grab your partner your energy either ends there or pulls back to you, making attempts at extension more difficult. When you combine the proper *te no uchi* that is required in weapons training with proper extension, then your throws, called *nage waza*, and pinning techniques, called *katame waza*, become much more effective.

The *bokken* and *jo* are simply alternative tools for discovering Aikido. Many, but not all, believe valuable insights into ourselves and Aikido principles can be gained through their practice. Some Aikido teachers believe they are indispensable; others insist they should be avoided entirely. Both are correct in their own approach and context, and deserve proper respect as such. You absolutely can learn about Aikido from weapons work, just as you can learn about Aikido by opening a jar or by observing nature. Everything can teach you about Aikido.

MULTIPLE ATTACKS

In Aikido we primarily practise with a single partner at a time. Every technique requires an awareness of that partner's full martial capabilities: can the other hand strike us; can they kick us; can they pull out a hidden weapon and reach us with it? Eventually, however, we must expand our awareness to include the possibility of several attackers. Multiple attack practice, or *randori*, requires us to take control of the space, the situation, to move quickly, efficiently, effectively and powerfully, maintaining a calm assertiveness throughout. A basic Aikido strategy handed down from O Sensei is to 'handle one as many and many as one'. Training with both a single opponent or multiple attackers give us the chance to put this theory into practice. *Randori* practice is an excellent vehicle to open up our awareness, and to develop effective body movement that combines mobility with stability.

Once blending with one of our partners we must move and control them to the extent that we neutralize any and all threats from them. We can control them and their balance by controlling their center. We can choose to throw them immediately or not. We can use one or more attackers as buffers against other attackers, even retaining the option of throwing them into the other attackers, if necessary.

Figure 14　*'Handle one as many and many as one'*
　　　　　　　　– Morihei Ueshiba

The full effectiveness of a multiple attack practice allows for an aikidoist to project an initial attacker into oncoming attackers. This becomes fairly easy to do and is considered the most basic skill level. This, of course, could result in potential injury to all. A higher level of expertise would be to take that first attacker and throw them in such a way that neither are they injured, nor do they injure anyone else, including the other attackers. You then demonstrate that your skills are such that you can still handle the other incoming attackers in the same manner – with speed, proficiency, effectiveness, calmness and compassion – while remaining in a centerd state throughout it all.

BASIC AIKIDO TECHNIQUES

Although the actual techniques of Aikido are limitless, I will cover some of the most basic and common. The following techniques are practically universal throughout the Aikido world. Some names may differ slightly, depending upon the particular Aikido organization, but the techniques themselves remain constant and widely accepted. The names do not matter; whether a technique is referred to as *iriminage* or *kokyunage* makes no difference to its performance.

All Aikido techniques can be practised vigorously or mildly; they can either take the opponent down close or project them a great distance. Many of these same techniques can be used to restrain or pin the opponent. Pinning techniques are called *kateme waza*.

Aikido techniques can be applied in two basic directions in relation to the opponent. *Omote waza* are techniques performed in front of the opponent; *Ura waza* are those performed behind the opponent. Many techniques have both an *omote* and *ura* application and variations.

Additionally there are two basic ways to move in Aikido: entering or turning. Entering is called *irimi* and turning is called *tenkan*. Therefore, the combination of the two movements is referred to as *irimi-tenkan* – to enter and turn.

Techniques can further be performed at three basic horizontal levels. The high level, called *jodan*, refers to techniques performed at the level of the chest and head. Middle level, or *chudan*, encompasses those performed at waist to chest level. Finally, the low level, or *gedan*, refers to applications lower than the waist.

Ikkyo – *First Teaching*

Ikkyo is the standard basic Aikido technique. Its application causes no pain and deals with controlling the opponent's

Figure 15 Ikkyo

center by holding and moving their extended arm. *Ikkyo* brings the opponent's arm down and pins it horizontally, flat on the ground. *Ikkyo* can be applied to virtually any type of attack, and can also be used as a projection technique.

Nikyo, *sankyo*, *yonkyo*, *gokyo* and *rokyo* (second, third, fourth, fifth and sixth techniques) are closely related to *ikkyo*. Some flow out of *ikkyo* applications. They can, therefore, be considered *henka waza*, when one switches from one technique to another. All these pinning techniques will bring the opponent to the ground and control him.

Iriminage – *Entering Throw*

With this classic Aikido technique, the opponent's energy is led up in front of their body and then down behind them to their rear. Some *iriminage* techniques enter directly into the opponent. Others involve entering, turning and unbalancing the opponent, then, as the opponent seeks to recover, leading them up and then down again for the final throw. *Iriminage* projects *uke* to the ground, allowing *nage* to remain standing. It finishes with *nage*'s palms facing down and towards the thrown *uke*.

Figure 16   Iriminage

Shihonage – *Four Direction Throw*

Shihonage is performed by extending the opponent's same arm using the gripping action of the *shihonage. Nage* then steps underneath *uke*'s extended arm and brings *uke*'s hand to *uke*'s same shoulder. The 'four directions' refers to the four basic directions to which *nage* can move in relation to *uke*. It also refers to the four basic directions in which *uke* can be thrown. However, as one masters the subtilties of *shihonage*, or any Aikido technique, one can move and throw in any direction. It is considered a high level, or *jodan* level, technique. *Shihonage* can be used to project the opponent away or pin him to the ground.

Figure 17   Shihonage

Kotegaeshi – *Wrist Turnout*

Kotegaeshi is a wrist-bending technique that takes the opponent to the ground and pins them with several variations of *kateme waza.* This technique is generally performed at a waist level, *chudan* level. It involves *nage* using both his hands in a specific method to apply the *kotegaeshi* to the *uke*'s one hand. This, again, is a technique where *uke* can be dramatically projected a distance.

Figure 18 Kotegaeshi

Kokyunage – *Breath Throw*

Kokyunage generally looks as though *nage* is picking up a large object, moving it a few feet, and setting it down again. When an opponent is drawn into this technique he is also projected to the ground as a result. *Kokyunage* can allow for a variety of head containments and traps, as well as other pins, chokes and arm bars. *Nage*'s palms face up upon completion of the basic projection. All Aikido techniques

Figure 19 Kokyunage

involve proper co-ordination of the breath and body, although *kokyunage* specifically calls special attention to these factors.

Tenchinage – *Heaven & Earth Throw*

The opponent has held *nage*'s wrists with both his hands in an attack called *ryotetori*. *Nage* extends one hand to earth and the other to the heavens, splitting *uke*'s attention and energy. *Tenchinage* projects *uke* to the ground and finishes similarly to *iriminage* with both *nage*'s palms down and towards the thrown *uke*.

Figure 20   Tenchinage

Koshinage – *Hip/Waist Throw*

Koshinage techniques seem to take *uke* across *nage*'s back. Specifically, *koshinage* takes *uke* over the lower back, or sacral area, of *nage*'s back. It differs from similar throws of other arts in that *nage* is able to remain standing upon its completion. Hence, having the ability to move, *nage* can make a quick exit or handle other attackers. *Koshinage* begins to benefit one's sense of what is behind one while developing an added awareness of the power and placement of the hips and center.

Figure 21 Koshinage

Ushiro Waza – *Techniques against Attacks from Behind*

Techniques performed against attacks from *nage*'s rear are called *ushiro waza*. *Ushiro* techniques are important for developing the mind's eye and gaining a kinetic and intuitive sense of the attacker. Panic can set in more easily when an attack is launched from behind. Therefore, *nage* practises

Figure 22 Ushiro Waza

maintaining composure while executing the techniques. Practically all of the above-mentioned techniques can be applied to attacks from *ushiro*.

Kokyu Dosa – *Breath-Developing Exercise*

This technique involves both partners sitting in *seiza*, facing each other, with knees practically touching. *Uke* holds onto both of *nage*'s wrists. *Nage* then practises co-ordinating his breath, grounding and body movement to uproot and unbalance *uke*. *Nage* then moves *uke* to the side and follows, using the same held hands to pin *uke*.

Figure 23   Kokyo Dosa

Suwari Waza – *Kneeling Techniques*

Suwari waza techniques are those performed from a seated or kneeling position. These techniques are generally performed while *nage* is up on his toes in a position referred to as 'live toes'. While in live toes, one or both of *nage*'s knees are in contact with the mat. With *suwari waza* one develops mobility of the hips while effectively moving one's center to complete the techniques. Practising a specific technique's *suwari waza* application can greatly enhance that technique's effectiveness when it is applied while standing. In addition, from a reflexology standpoint, *suwari waza* opens up and stimulates the entire body through reflex points in the feet and toes.

Figure 24   Suwari Waza

Hanmi Handachi – *Kneeling Techniques against Standing Opponents*

Hanmi handachi takes the mobility gained with standard *suwari waza* practice and expands on it, increasing the distance of its effectiveness (*see* page 83). Being able to perform techniques while on one's knees ensures controlled, expansive movement when those techniques are brought into standing practices.

Randori – *Freestyle Techniques against Multiple Attackers*

Randori practice enables the Aikido practitioner to flow quickly, and move efficiently, from one attacker to the next. It is generally considered the epitomy of Aikido training and is often the culmination of many upper-rank testing requirements.

Figure 25   Hanmi Handachi

A final note: all these are but a few of the most basic Aikido techniques. Other common ones are: *Tachi-tori*, *Jo-tori* and *Tanto-tori* (weapons disarming), *Sumi-otoshi* (corner drop), *Udegarame* (arm containment), *Udekimenage* (arm projection), *Kaitenage* (rotary throw) and *Jujinage* (crossed-arm throw). The list is endless.

TRIANGLE, CIRCLE & SQUARE

Three graphic elements commonly associated with representing Aikido are the triangle, circle and square. There are many interpretations for them, from simply showing the variety inherent in Aikido to the more esoteric cosmic references of, for instance, the Omoto-Kyo religion and the *kotodama* theories it espouses (*see* pages 14–15).

Because these three symbols are referred to in so many different contexts and since there are many explanations, I'll keep it simple and cover their relationship to Aikido only briefly: basically speaking, the triangle represents assertiveness and focus, the circle fluidity and the square stability.

An Aikido technique begins with an entering movement, or *irimi*, into our opponent's center. The triangle represents this *irimi*. The technique continues with a spiral blending

*Figure 26   Aikido techniques can be used to throw one or more
attackers simultaneously.*

and joining, called *musubi*. The conjoined movement with
the opponent is represented by the circle. Finally, upon
completion of the technique we return to stability and solidity, represented by the square. This is an explanation for an
elementary breakdown of basic focus and energy awareness.

As experience and awareness increase these elements are
actually present simultaneously at any given point: for
example, having both fluidity and stability when entering;
or finishing with stability yet entering and blending with
whatever may be around us through our awareness, as a
result of our *zanshin*, or mindfulness.

7 · BENEFITS OF AIKIDO TRAINING

Understand Aikido first as budo and then as a way of service to construct the World Family.

– Morihei Ueshiba

Ask any one of the million aikidoists in the world today to describe what they get from Aikido and they will probably reply with first one benefit, then another, and another, until they realize they are at a loss for words. The benefits, some obvious and some less so, received from Aikido training are many and deep.

Aikido agrees with, and uses, the power of peace, acceptance, understanding and compassion. Many practices, approaches and beliefs, therefore, enhance Aikido and vice versa. It is an enriching activity that brings everyone to a healthier state of living and being; it lifts the unhealthy and healthy alike to new levels.

AIKIDO & HOLISTIC HEALTH

O Sensei said that all of Aikido is *misogi*, meaning purification. Aikido is self-purification at every level. How is this possible? It is because Aikido training challenges the practitioner's physical capabilities, mental capacities, range of emotion and quality of spirit.

Aikido can challenge anyone, regardless of age, size or gender. It can also be tempered to a moderate, low or even non-impact level, depending upon the individual's skill level, age or inclination. Because it can be adjusted in this way, allowing for factors such as age, physical limitations or disabilities, its benefits can be enjoyed by everyone.

The physical training of Aikido develops better posture; deeper, more open, more controlled and effective breathing; increased flexibility, without sacrificing strength and resiliency; practical self-defence capabilities; and much more. Aikido opens, strengthens and enriches the body and the mind. Aikido's natural movements, whether done vigorously or slowly, promote healthier circulation. Circulation is improved by both the opening up of the body as well as the conditioning effect of Aikido activity. Respiratory capacity increases because of the focus given to the power of the breath combined with the exercise levels inherent in Aikido.

A relaxed yet vibrant body is favoured in Aikido. This encourages constricted muscles to open, expand and elongate, further opening up the entire body and stretching those muscles, ligaments and tendons. The capillaries' capacity to cleanse and resupply the body with its nutrients is increased. A constricted body can not only inhibit blood flow, but also impede the lymphatic system and the important cleansing accomplished by it.

As one begins Aikido there is a period of learning and adjustment where one may have to slow the technique down in order to see and know where one's feet, hands and body should be directed. As progress is made the training can become increasingly aerobic, if that is what the individual desires. At the more intense and advanced levels of practice, Aikido can be very aerobically challenging and invigorating. As with any aerobic activity this releases endorphins, creating the natural 'runner's high' one gets from such exercise. Even the simplest back-and-forth rolls of Aikido *ukemi* massage, relax, open up and strengthen the spine and the abdomen. Good posture requires good abdominal muscles. Aikido rolls, in addition to all Aikido techniques and movements, develop such strength and tone while increasing suppleness throughout the entire body.

When first introduced to Aikido, students may be surprised by the sudden pain that can be applied in some of Aikido's basic techniques. They are often stunned that such an effect can result from such a simple action. They are even more perplexed when they see that as soon as the technique is released the pain is alleviated. Any pain created by a good Aikido technique is momentary and for motivational purposes only, without causing damage. A properly performed Aikido wrist technique, for example, will take the largest person to the ground, yet causes no harm.

Because Aikido techniques are simple, yet can be so devastatingly effective, they must be applied with full awareness of our partners. If any pain is experienced by our *ukes* during application of a properly executed technique, it is momentary and is gone as soon as the technique is accomplished and released. Just as we can all experience a 'good' as opposed to a 'bad' pain, such as in a massage, the bending and natural twisting of joints with Aikido technique should feel good. A technique performed on a partner's hand will affect the status of the entire body right down to the toes. Every point along that path will be stretched and massaged as a result. One prominent Aikido master describes it as 'cleaning out the joints'. Many claim that this increased flexibility has even been successful in alleviating symptoms of arthritis that they had had prior to Aikido.

On a mental level, Aikido requires the unification of both the right and left hemispheres of the brain, bringing into balance both the intellect and intuition. Studies long ago found that the left hemisphere of the brain is the center for our intellectual and analytical powers. It gives us the ability to analyze the martial, ethical and spiritual aspects of each Aikido technique, direct our bodies and minds through it and explain it to both ourselves and others. The right brain is the center for our intuition, creativity and spontaneity. In Aikido, it allows for these traits to bloom and provides insights into movement, timing and connection. In Aikido, when the right brain is stuck, the left brain can help. When the left brain is stranded, the right brain can come to the rescue. Because we are what we are, both must be acknowledged and balanced. A productive partnership can be created.

In order to maximize success with Aikido one must develop a balanced emotional state. Letting emotions such as anger and fear rule our state of mind can affect our centeredness; and that, naturally, affects how well we perform our Aikido. They can lock up our bodies either in part or on the whole. Accepting these emotions (as we would our attacking partner) and examining their effects allows us to learn about them. We can then control them better at their source – deep in our own psyche.

Our emotional state can greatly affect both our physical and mental states. If our emotional, physical and mental states are affected, our spirit is next in line. So, you see, if *any* state is affected then *every* state is affected. We are integrated beings and our job is to make it a healthy integration. If we are upset, for example, we are distracted, so our awareness suffers. Being upset, the body begins to contract, even collapse, making it unable to respond to its needs for, say, good posture. We find it harder to focus, to concentrate, to be in control – to be centered. Take this state into Aikido practice and it can quickly lead to panic and over-reaction.

Getting your center back allows everything else to fall into place, and takes back the power that emotion controlled. Being centered better enables you to put things into perspective. Your ability to react comfortably and more effectively is not compromised. Your ability to see clearly is not clouded. Your ability to be compassionate is not inhibited.

Because of the nature of Aikido and the introspection and awareness it requires, one becomes acutely aware of imbalances, whether they be in posture, mental or emotional states, diet or attitude. Since recognition of a problem is the first stage in solving it, we then have the chance to make a change for the better: to fine-tune our balance; to achieve a more peaceful state of being.

We are all seeking peace. Where does that desire come from? It comes from our spirit. The spirit longs for it. Our spirit wishes to bring peace to all our levels and beyond. With Aikido we can say to our spirit, 'Here is a way to peace.' Aikido acknowledges, invigorates and soothes the mind, the emotions and the spirit, as well as the body. It does this by both opening them up and increasing their resilience at the same time.

Another important side benefit of Aikido is the people who are attracted to it. The Aikido *dojo* is a community of like-minded individuals from all walks of life. The camaraderie experienced in the *dojo* offers a support system of people who are caring and peace-loving. I have always said that I think Aikido attracts the best of people. They tend to be friendly, kind, gracious, gregarious, generous, humane, gentle, sincere, affectionate, sympathetic, empathetic, benevolent, loving, forgiving, responsible, loyal, courageous and compassionate; and they can often combine a high calibre of character with a high degree of natural wisdom and intelligence. I am honoured and blessed to have the opportunity to be inspired by these people.

Because of Aikido's popularity and the quality of people who practise it, you can travel to any Aikido *dojo* in the world and have instant friends and acceptance. You can practise Aikido there with them in much the same manner as you do at your home *dojo*. And you would find they even use the same, now universal, terms for the Aikido techniques that you are familiar with.

FEELING GOOD

When we feel good about ourselves we interact with others more effectively. Most people prefer and enjoy being around happy people. If someone, as we say, walks in and 'lights up' the room, it is because the attitude of joy and happiness they exude has affected everyone there. Conversely, if that person was in a dour mood they would tend to bring others down as well. We have the capability at any moment to be led in a direction not exactly of our own choosing. Alternatively, we can be more conscious of these subliminal effects and choose not to go along with them.

The ripple effect is always present. In essence, everyone you affect goes on to affect ten more, and they will affect ten more, and so on. You can and do change the world whether you believe it or not. When you work to improve yourself you are 'acting locally' in the truest sense of the phrase. Who you are and what you do has both an immediate and long-range effect. Making changes in ourselves and, through that ripple effect, our extended environment actually works to bring about positive change globally. So, you see, you are already a pretty powerful person.

To be effective at Aikido and in life you must sometimes make a personal attitude adjustment. You must exercise your ability to choose and turn a negative attitude into a positive one. Others may want to help, may try to lead you to optimism, but you are the one who has to make it happen. Presence and centering can help. If you want to get out of a negative mood, sit or stand up straight, take a deep full breath and let it go; then take a positive course of action, take control by getting out of your worries – and help someone else. Try this on the Aikido mat and in your daily life.

Sometimes the most selfish thing you can do is to act selflessly. The reward you get from helping someone else builds a strong foundation for your own deep happiness. But it must always be from selflessness, with no expectation of any return for yourself. If you do it expecting some kind of reward you are missing the mark. When you think your situation is bad, remember that there are always plenty of others much worse off than you. Just take a look around you. Have you seen the news lately? Take it all into consideration. It should allow you to put things into better perspective and to gain some degree of balance. This may not seem to help when you are in the 'thick of it', but you have the choice to change your approach and come at it from another angle. Try a new tack.

These are the very same abilities and traits you must develop in order to be an exceptional aikidoist – just as they are necessary for effective and happy living. You must be able to instantly flow into alternatives. You must be comfortable with the discomfort of change. You must have patience with your impatience. You must endeavour to remain in positive control throughout it all. You must endeavour to sense another's intent, feel their heart, then guide them with powerful benevolence while keeping vigil on your own inner peace. You may then find that someone else, perhaps someone you may even dislike, has the same aspirations as yourself.

The joy of life comes from our accomplishments: our first steps into our parents' open arms; the exhilaration of a challenging ski run; the joy that comes from seeing someone else's life improved by a simple selfless act we did. We are driven to better ourselves. We do not have a choice – it is our nature. Whether it be personal grooming, our golf stroke or our 'station in life', we naturally seek improvement. We must evolve, both as individuals and as a species. It is ingrained in our nature. We must guide this trait carefully in order to continue as an ever-evolving species enjoying this garden planet. This desire to improve and this planet are gifts. The former is *what* we are; the latter is *where* we are. We should use our natural desire to improve, along with our wisdom and intelligence, to enhance both ourselves and the planet we live on. Aikido gives us a forum to bring out our best qualities.

INTUITION & INSTINCT

Absence of evidence is not evidence of absence.

Anon

Intuition and instinct are natural abilities. They cannot be measured. The evidence of their existence is within us. These wonderful gifts and the valuable information they bring are too often ignored, even ridiculed. Likewise, we are taught that being afraid is an undesirable trait, but fear is one of our greatest gifts. It is a wonderful siren for self-preservation as well as self-defence. It warns us of danger and cautions us as we navigate through it. It can whisk us away to safety through instinctual survival reactions. It is the healthy acceptance and recognition of fear that enables the climber to survive the mountain, the sailor to survive the sea, the pedestrian to survive the streets. These are a few of the most important tools for both good self-defence and a good life. For eons we have relied on them. They are, combined with our intelligence, the reason we have survived as a species. They are part of our nature, and must be acknowledged and trusted; they should be used, not repressed.

The practice of Aikido develops and even requires sensitivity. And sensitivity is closely tied to intuition. Intuition is closely tied to us.

You don't have to try to use intuition; it is there all the time. You just have to listen to its voice. When confronted by someone, whether we know them or not, we may intuit, or sense, if something is not quite right. Discomfort is the first sign that requires your attention. The closer the physical proximity, the stronger the feeling may be – the knowing. You can feel it through the space between you. The real threat of physical harm increases as physical distance decreases. Discomfort, fear's early warning system, increases. Your psychic radar signals increase in frequency and bounce back to you, bringing their warning with increased urgency. Once physical contact is made, the intuitive connection should be complete. If there was doubt before, then contact either removes it or makes everything much clearer. Unfortunately, in the case of a physical attack, waiting for the physical contact may mean you have waited too long. Intuition and instinct could save you.

A victim of a physical assault will often give statements such as 'I had a feeling . . .' or 'I knew in my gut . . . '. How often have you and I said the same thing, thankful that we heeded its voice or regretting we did not? This valuable intuitive information too often goes unheeded. In the case of crime victims, they may have known, through their intuition, and its siren – fear – what someone's true intent was. They may not have acted on their intuition or, if they did, they may have acted too late. Recognizing these signals and trusting them is one of the first major steps in mastering Aikido.

Through Aikido training we learn to recognize the approach of our partner's mind, intent, energy and spirit; to trust in our intuition; to listen to our fear signals; to use our instincts properly and to move and respond accordingly.

THE QUALITY OF TOUCH

Aikido can only be learned by having physical contact with a practice partner.

Once you make physical contact with your partner the quality of that touch will have a profound effect on the inter-action. If you grab strongly, with force, your partner may seize up in a reflex action. Your attempts to lead them will be resisted or stopped entirely. However, if you hold them gently, yet firmly, from your core, they feel a certain security. They can feel your caring. They know, through their own intuition, where your mind and heart are. They trust you because of it and are much more prone to co-operate with your leading. They do not resist because they do not feel you as a threat. They do not feel your urgency because you have none. With this touch it is possible to heal a frightened soul.

We all respond positively to a gentle touch just as we all respond strongly if grabbed with force. We know through our intuition if the touch is based in caring, respect and compassion, or if it is a ruse. We all have been held gently as babies. That memory and the comfort and security it brings is pro-grammed deeply in our internal make-up. Our psyche responds naturally to the mothering care it brings and our mind and body follow suit. We will co-operate with a gentle touch much more than a forceful one. Advanced Aikido enables us to develop that quality of touch, learn its wisdom and carry those same principles into our lives.

A common mistake when coming to Aikido is to think the technique is performed at whatever point you are grabbed. When we are grabbed, our own attention and our energy gets drawn to that spot. We trap ourselves. As we try to force the technique from this grab our partner is immediately aware of our effort and naturally resists it to lesser or, the more we force it, even greater degrees. Your agenda and your urgency can be felt. The actual grab, as it turns out, distracts us from where the technique is really performed. All Aikido techniques originate from, and are performed and accomplished by, the movement of our centers and the subtle, yet powerful co-operation of the hips and lower body. If you keep your hands passive and perform your Aikido technique with the rest of your body, allowing all the joints to absorb and conduct all the energy, you will successfully perform that technique.

In order to gain trust you must prove that you warrant it. People, generally, will not automatically trust anyone who comes along, especially when engaged in a physical activity such as a potentially dangerous martial art. In these close quarters you must prove through your character and actions that you can be honoured with your partner's trust. Your intentions are easily evidenced in the quality of your touch. If the proper quality of physical contact is made it can have a profound affect on your partner. He feels your friendship; he feels your caring and honouring. It feels good to him because it is good. This cannot be faked; if it is, it won't work for long. Lies are short-lived. Truth endures. You must cultivate and then exhibit this level of integrity in order to reap the benefits of Aikido training.

Aikido comes from a place where a simple touch, from the proper source and given in the proper manner, can create immense healing, and in the giving can heal the healer as well.

HUMOUR & INTENSITY

We all want to have fun. When we are encouraged to have a good time and have fun we are more comfortable. We relax. When we are relaxed we become more open, more receptive. We can even begin to be more forgiving – even to ourselves – when the time comes to face our own mistakes.

In a healthy Aikido practice atmosphere, students can make the transition between humour and smiling to sharp focus and intense concentration easily and instantaneously. This is a skill necessary for enjoying life while still being able to focus immediately and fully when the need arises. When a serious danger pops up, often suddenly and without warning, we must have the ability to respond quickly, efficiently and effectively.

When seeking out a good Aikido teacher who encourages a serious yet enjoyable learning environment think back to your school days. Which teachers created the best, most relaxed, yet stimulating educational atmosphere? Discipline and mutual respect, certainly, have to be part of a learning environment. And so it is in a martial art, such as Aikido, where there is a potential for injury. There must also be guidelines to maintain safety. However, there are few willing to continue learning in such an environment if it is too harsh or too rigid. Many people come to Aikido already having experienced the harsh rigours of other arts and disciplines. A large percentage even have an extensive background in another martial art. They are attracted to Aikido because they seek to further evolve their capabilities. They may also have matured in their knowledge of the 'ways of the world'. Prior martial art experience, I should mention, is not necessary to study and be accomplished at Aikido. It can be of help in some cases and be a hindrance in others. Aikido can be a challenge for all and it accepts all comers.

As Aikido proficiency in both technique and *ukemi* is gained, two *aikidoka* practising together can be extremely intense, stretching the boundaries of their reaction times and execution abilities. It is a remarkable thing for the unfamiliar to see advanced aikidoists fully engaged in advanced practice. They are moving so quickly, throwing so effortlessly, responding so naturally, yet no one is being injured. In fact, the aikidoists are thoroughly enjoying themselves, as evidenced by their smiles and the palpable joy emanating from them. The visitor sees dramatic throws where even the one taking the fall, sometimes even after being thrown through the air 15 or 20ft, gets up unhurt and, smiling, rushes back for more! Visitors ask, 'Why aren't they getting hurt? Doesn't that hurt? Are you sure?' They just can't believe their eyes. This is possible because of the inspired nature of Aikido's techniques and the practitioners' skills, combined with the proper atmosphere of safety, mutual respect, responsible discipline and joy.

Intensity opens the door to instinctive and intuitive reaction. It brings a strength and sharpness to the spirit, and mobilizes the mind into sharp focus. Developing the ability to move effortlessly between humour and intensity will go a long way in improving your centering response time and strengthening your capacity for both.

Good Aikido technique results in both partners smiling and healthy at the end of the technique, despite the level of intensity. If we learn to take that quality of responsiveness and responsibility into the other events and moments of our lives, maybe we'd hurt less and be even more effective – both inwardly and outwardly.

CONFIDENCE

All martial arts training leads, certainly, to increased confidence. To be self-assured and assertive when appropriate are natural by-products of responsible training. Confidence, if not tempered, may lead to over-confidence, and over-confidence invites, even begs for, disaster. Proper training in Aikido, or any art, should encourage the development of wisdom, common sense, mature awareness and sensible caution in order to bring about a deeper, more meaningful, true confidence that has no need of boasting or proclamation or even recognition.

Being over-confident can cause just as many problems as having a lack of confidence. On the street, if you appear weak, nervous, frightened and unsure of yourself, you are advertising yourself as a prime victim for a predator. At the same time, if you walk down the street with an air of over-confidence or arrogance, ignoring obvious signals of trouble, then there are plenty of people who would like to 'cut you down to size'. You can actually be exuding a challenge, pushing your presence into other psyches that would love to push back, or worse. Keeping yourself in balance and maintaining a comfortable, self-assured state will allow you to be neither the victim nor the challenger. This balanced state, then, gives you the option to consciously choose an appearance of weakness or over- confidence. This option can be a valuable strategy in times of need. True confidence needs no advertising, nor does it seek it. True confidence simply is.

When one preys on those who are weaker, they have given birth to the bully. As we all know, bullies are not limited to the school playground. Unhappy, out-of-balance people who feel powerless seek to elevate themselves into a position of power by distressing and controlling others. The energy exchange can be an interesting one. It may be that misery does, indeed, love company, and if it cannot find it, then it will create it. If the bully, or those who are unhappy, can make someone else miserable too, then they are no longer alone. Those who are unhappy are envious of happiness. The knowledge that they do not have it strikes deep. It brings attention to the wound; the wound caused by feeling they are unheard, unappreciated, unseen, unloved.

Originally, I was attracted to *karate* for the self-discipline and self-control it would give me, besides it being a more efficient vehicle for my hands and feet. I thought that if I knew better how to use them, I would gain some control and relax further with an increased confidence in my ability to tolerate. Still, at times I found myself being confronted with the possibility of a fight through no intention or desire on my part. I just happened to be at the wrong place when something decided to go down. Fortunately, in each of those times, because I kept a cool head stayed on the edge but didn't go over it, and used reasoning and my verbal skills, the confrontations never escalated. I was deeply disturbed, nonetheless, because all my *karate* training was geared to breaking through the opponent's sternum for a decisive blow – one that could result in that person's death or serious injury. I had no inclination to respond with such severity. These were not life-and-death situations, so killing or maiming the other person in order to stop them were totally outrageous alternatives. If I hadn't diffused the situation, however, my physical response would have been, undoubtedly, automatic and regrettable. I was a peaceful person, yet I felt I had a lethal ability that could not be 'put on stun'. If I acted it was going to be with severe consequences. All or nothing. Aikido changed all that.

If attacked, I wanted the ability to handle the attack without injuring the attacker. I wanted increased awareness skills. I wanted to get in better touch with, and trust more, my intuitive abilities. I wanted to find out more about myself and others. I wanted control. I wanted peace. Aikido was my answer. I found that Aikido offers a limitless range of response and endless degrees of appropriateness. I saw that Aikido offers true confidence.

MAINTAINING CONTROL

A friend of mine in the *dojo* is a pilot and often takes me flying. It's always a learning experience and a challenge for me. I have always been prone to motion sickness while flying. I look at each flight with him as an opportunity to learn about, and possibly control, this fear. I've observed that I do not fare too well handling the dips and turns, especially the more dramatic they become. But once he allows me to take over flying the plane it all changes for me. *Ah, I'm in control now!* I have the subtle advantage of knowing what is happening and being able to control the adjustments necessary to keep going along smoothly. Like my Aikido practice, I'm in the moment – feeling, adjusting, searching, actively involved in the responsibility of finding harmony and comfort – even if a part of me isn't too comfortable at the time.

In striving for control, I hope to tolerate my insecurity and have patience with my impatience.

There is an adage that states there are three kinds of people in the world: those who make things happen; those who watch things happen; and those who wonder what the heck happened. In Aikido, if you find yourself merely watching what happens, you are going to wind up wondering what the heck happened. You must be an active participant. You must move, engage, blend and become actively involved. You must make things happen. That requires fine-tuning and exercising your abilities to adjust and control.

In our Aikido practice we learn to maintain control even when giving it up – *especially* by giving it up – no matter what role we are practising. Interestingly, whether we are practising the Aikido technique or taking *ukemi* (giving the attack and receiving the Aikido technique while smoothly, gracefully and comfortably surviving it), we practise towards having that ability. Both *nage* and *uke* share a 'letting-go' process – giving up their positions and expectations. Both must go into the technique by giving up these expectations. *Nage* must give up his space and status to some degree in order to blend with the attack and redirect it. *Uke* must give up his expectation of a successful attack in order to absorb the technique and survive it comfortably and safely. Therefore, *nage* does not vanquish, but rather blends and maintains. *Uke* does not lose, but rather absorbs and recovers. To the uninitiated *nage* may seem to be the winner and *uke* the loser, but, as you can see, Aikido allows and encourages both to be winners.

Human beings are a very adaptable species. With familiarity and practice we adjust and learn, eventually becoming comfortable with even some of the most severe challenges and circumstances. It is remarkable that as individuals, and as a species, we can be so talented, so gifted, so intelligent, yet we can be so lacking as well. For instance, we are familiar with DNA, space travel, eons of geological history and so much more. Yet even after decades of enlightened legislation and 'public awareness' we continue to pollute and destroy the very planet we depend on for our existence. We continue to be, as in the words of Tom Brown Jr's mentor, Stalking Wolf, an Apache elder, 'a people that kill our grandchildren to feed our children'.

Practising Aikido shows us that we do, indeed, share responsibility for many and maybe even all outcomes. It brings our role, and the power we have with it, into focus. It shows us that we are not merely watching from the sidelines, but we are interwoven into everything that goes on around us. We can maintain control even when it seems we have relinquished it. Change is perennially inevitable. But to a large degree we must already be comfortable with change, otherwise we would never have reached the hunter/gatherer stage. We can create change, and we can affect it when it is thrust upon us. We can responsibly create a new outcome, possibly one not even anticipated beforehand.

PERSONAL POWER

Studying Aikido, and gaining the security and options it brings, empowers you. We all seek power whether we consciously admit it to ourselves or not. The power to have control over our situation, over our lives. When you don't feel powerful, you don't feel in control. You can feel ineffective, frustrated, unrespected, even unloved. You may feel you have lost your dignity. You may feel you are a failure.

In a healthy Aikido *dojo* you are encouraged to acknowledge your accomplishments: to not only focus on how far you have to go, but on how far you have already come; to take pride in both; to keep a balance, and feel the personal power you have. This does not mean the 'wow, I can kick butt now' kind of power. That type of power is superficial at best. The kind of power I'm referring to is the kind that *can* destroy, but has the strength of character *not to*. The former may be feared by all, the latter deeply felt and respected by all. The former is envied by those who can't really feel their own power. The latter inspires those who know that they, too, possess the same potential inner strength. Those who use bravado, aggression, threats and violence are actually demonstrating their feeling of being powerless. This behaviour can, paradoxically, be a sign of insecurity and inner fear.

For example, we do not want police who take out their weapons at the slightest indication of difficulty. We require them to have the strength of character to use restraint, to mediate and to restore the peace without resorting to violence. We should expect the same from ourselves. Experienced and responsible law enforcement officers may not be familiar with Aikido's physical technique (though more and more are turning to Aikido), but they can have a good working knowledge of Aikido principles.

Figure 27   Aikido techniques do not destroy but promote life.

In Aikido many of your existing powers are pointed out – for instance, your ability to choose may be, arguably, your most powerful. For example, the teacher will point out where strikes may be applicable throughout the Aikido technique. These strikes are called *atemi waza* and are generally meant to distract your partner's attention so that you can continue through the technique. These strikes do not necessarily make contact, but are merely feints. They can, however, give you the capability of inflicting harm if necessary. Knowing you have this power you then have the option to continue through with the technique with a more ethical alternative. This has the benefit of additionally empowering you. You have the power to destroy, but you also have the opportunity to become admirably more powerful by choosing not to. However, having that power you are now comfortable to continue with the full Aikido technique while exercising the personal choice of a more ethical outcome. There is a paradox in the best Aikido technique that by taking care not to injure the attacker, we are actually putting ourselves in the safest position, handling even larger opponents and gaining the capability of fully controlling them and dissipating their attacks, without incurring harm to either yourself or them. Aikido techniques and principles offer peaceful alternatives for all.

8 • AIKIDO AS A WAY OF LIFE

The highest art is the art of living an ordinary life in an extraordinary manner.

– Tibetan saying

AIKIDO & YOUR PERSONAL EVOLUTION

Aikido is, undeniably, an amazing martial art at the very least, and an extremely effective means of dealing with a physical attack. The greatest enemy many of us will ever face, however, is the one inside our own mind and the psyche behind it. Precious few of us meet this foe with our full potential. The chances of running into a physical attack that would require us to use actual Aikido techniques will, hopefully, be slim – if ever. The real value of Aikido, therefore, is in what it does for our character and the everyday quality of our lives. Aikido is both life training and training *for* life.

Aikido training is a fully integrated method of self-discovery. Its physical practice requires our full attention in order to experience the joy of successful Aikido technique. Regular training develops the same qualities necessary to enjoy and maintain effective living, and brings out and develops these qualities and ingrains them deeply into our character.

While practising on the mat, we need to co-ordinate our mind, body and spirit. In order to control our body we must, then, control our mind because it is the mind that moves the body. In order to control our mind we must, finally, control our spirit because it is the spirit that moves the mind.

On the mat we are shown how we have been programmed by past experience and culture to react and respond. This on-the-mat interaction is a tangible manifestation of that programming. In other words, when confronted with a per-ceived difficulty, do we fight, freeze, flee or simply freak out? These are well-researched and documented basic human responses, and any or all of them can be valid, depending upon circumstance, so long as they are consciously used from a standpoint of a stable, peaceful mind in a centerd state. When we feel that we cannot adequately control these responses, our internal peace is disturbed. When we are caught up in these responses, we often do not see the other choices we have. Our habitual reactions become our only real-ity. Aikido offers alternative realities, and points out other prospects and possibilities. With the enlightenment of other quite viable options, we can begin to reprogramme the undesirable, or outmoded behaviour patterns and responses that are working *against* us instead of *for* us.

Aikido is a wonderful tool for finding out how to create and maintain inner peace from moment to moment. It reveals how we relate and interact to others, and makes it easier to both understand them and ourselves. It teaches us how to better guide and control our own responses. Aikido gives us the ability to feel better about ourselves and others; it allows us to be more forgiving of our own shortcomings, mistakes and behaviour as well as those of others.

Good Aikido requires good leadership skills. A good leader must be balanced, fair, intelligent, courageous, of strong char-acter, be able to handle responsibility, be able to see the big picture, and provide vision. A good leader inspires others by example; motivates; takes charge; and makes decisions for the good of all. Other attributes include a good sense of humour, compassion and wisdom. A good leader, like a good aikidoist, is someone whom others willingly follow.

A calm, unruffled demeanour is ideal for optimum Aikido performance and also for enjoyable living. Aikido training can give us the insights into our own behaviour that are necessary to better handle the internal forces that inhibit our own happiness. You will find that you can blend with an attack and effortlessly redirect that energy without sacrificing your internal or external balance. Simultaneously, you can reprogramme your behaviour repertoire with what you will find is a better way.

Aikido, as a method of both self-defence and self-exploration, opens up new worlds, new possibilities. It can illuminate the many paths that lead us away from the dangers of despair, frustration, fear, hate, arrogance and pain.

CONNECTION & THE JOY OF AIKIDO

Aikido is a way to reconcile the world and make human beings one family.

– Morihei Ueshiba

To quote from the *dojo* rules posted at Aikido World Headquarters in Tokyo, 'Aikido should be practised at all times with a feeling of pleasurable exhilaration.' It makes sense. If you want to enjoy anything, go into it with exuberance and maintain a joyous manner.

To be successful in Aikido one must practise with joy and enthusiasm in order to accomplish the goal of good technique and discover the true heart of the art. To enjoy life, shouldn't we approach it in the same manner? When we feel happy, we feel better connected to everything around us. We feel we are more integrated. Conversely, when we are unhappy, we feel disconnected. We feel alone, separate from and strangers to the world around us. We need to feel connected. We need the acceptance that connection brings to us. Aikido requires that we connect with others; and see ourselves in them; and rejoice in that discovery.

We all crave connection. It is the make-up of ourselves and our society. We band together in cliques, groups, organizations, armies, gangs and social clubs to feel that we are accepted; to feel that we belong. If you agree with Groucho Marx when he said, 'I would never belong to a club that would have me as a member', then you are either being brutally honest about your character, or you are not seeing yourself clearly at all.

In Aikido we need to create and maintain a deep connection to our practice partners for our technique to be most effective. We must acknowledge their presence and then their intent. We must feel their hearts. We must make that connection and maintain it throughout the entire interaction – especially if you want to soothe 'the savage beast'. It is not only music that can accomplish this. In Aikido practice, good connection and touch will have the same effect. Aikido traits of compassion and responsibility are important for our practice partner. We must do all this while keeping our own equilibrium and peaceful state of mind.

We find that our techniques work much better when we do not use force. From birth till death, no one likes being forced to do anything. As *nage*, we must blend with the attacker in order to redirect and guide them. If *nage* tries to use force, *uke* will not co-operate. Force is not the most effective method of leading. In combining connection with the right quality of touch, we are more agreeable to our partners. We can lead them, move them, through co-operation. Aikido is less about insistence, more about polite suggestions from an unwavering, strong, yet benevolent character. In this way our partner is joined and redirected most efficiently.

Aikido's physical techniques are effective tools for transformation; and, like most tools, must be used properly. Irresponsible practice can damage you and/or your partners. Improper practice can injure the body, harm the mind and destroy the spirit. It can either build up or break down both you and your partners. You have a say in which way it goes.

Aikido technique is like guiding a knife through bread. One must pay attention, have respect for the danger and direction of the knife, yet remain present and in control; for it cares not what it cuts. It is merely doing what you direct it to do, whether you are conscious of it or not. *You* give it animation and life. *You* are doing the cutting. *You* must do the caring. Otherwise you, too, can be cut.

When you make proper, healthy connections with your partners, they will feel seen, acknowledged, accepted and respected. Feeling respected, they are much more open to your leading. When any of us feel we have been heard, we are more likely to listen. If you are talking to someone you can sense when they are merely listening; you can tell if they are not paying attention – if they are not present. You know what depth of hearing and understanding – what level of connection – they are making with you. When you feel that you are not being heard, you probably feel like your opinion doesn't really matter. Do you feel like co-operating then? Probably not. If you feel you are truly being heard and respected, you are more likely to listen to another's point of view as well. You are more willing to co-operate. Everyone needs to feel that their opinions matter, that they matter. It is even better when they *know* they matter. They will get that from you if you believe it as well. You must develop the skills of a seasoned negotiator or mediator, to be able to agree with their intent; and, at the same time, feel that you have not lost but gained.

Likewise, the quality and depth of your connection and compassion to your partner will determine how good your Aikido will be. If you attempt to do your technique without this connection, your partner will know this. The lines of communication necessary for the best execution of the Aikido technique need to be established. Connection completes that circuit. Once the proper connection is made, you can feel if your partners are nervous, unsure, angry, distracted or distrustful. You may even sense if they are concerned about an undisclosed injury. It is, of course, very possible that you can execute a technique without regard to the level of connection. This will not be the best or most effective way to apply the technique; real Aikido goes deeper. It requires more interpersonal commitment. It requires true caring and kindness from the heart.

107

Aikido brings out these much-desired qualities while, paradoxically, developing a powerful means of self-defence. We develop our bodies, our minds, our psyches and our spirits while having fun practising with our Aikido partners. For many of us Aikido practice rekindles the joy of childhood play. At the same time, we acquire new options for better living with better connections to the world around us.

AIKIDO – LIFE TRAINING

To understand everything is to forgive everything.

– Buddha

Becoming accomplished at Aikido requires one to experience ongoing practice with a wide range of individuals. It demands interaction with varying, complex personalities and expectations, and the honing of one's skill in blending with their minds, bodies, spirits and hearts. Ideally, we learn to acknowledge and accept all others while not sacrificing ourselves. This can sound like quite a challenge, considering the great diversity of individuals in the world. But we must recognize that all that they are capable of – *we* are capable of – from extreme cruelty to unquestioning love. We have in our own personalities all others. There are no differences – only perceptions and expressions. The sooner one knows this, the sooner the barrier to blending and acceptance evaporates.

When we feel we are in control, anything and everything takes on a whole new experience. Again, we feel our power. And which of us does not want to be in control of, at least, our own life? We are, of course, never in 'control'; we simply adjust to the changes that constantly present themselves. The more we learn to give up the attachment to controlling our lives and/or our life situations, the more in control we actually are. Going with the flow, adjusting comfortably to the big and little changes that pop up, is how a well-adjusted, vital person maintains control. It is how an accomplished Aikidoist moves through powerful technique. Control, then, takes on new meaning. We maintain our balance, our equilibrium – our center. Someone, apparently, once asked the founder of Aikido, 'Sensei, do you ever lose your center?' His answer was 'Yes, all the time, but I get it back so fast that no one notices.'

The reality is that we have absolutely no control over anything other than ourselves. And even this is a formidable assignment. No matter what situation we find ourselves in, we have the potential to 'right' ourselves. Granted, some situations require more personal fortitude than others, but 'variety is the spice of life': we like variety. We enjoy the subtle nuances, flavours and challenges it offers.

You can choose to give up your ability to see options but, regardless of the severity of the storm, you always have them. Sometimes they may seem to be only negative. That can be a trap that will spiral you down into despair and pessimism. Survivors are possibility thinkers. Keep looking for the positive options; you may not see them right away, but they are there. Much depends on your perception. You have a choice to change it. Aikido can give you the tools to make it happen.

There is an old tale: an old man sat outside the walls of a great city. When travellers approached they would ask him, 'What kind of people live in this city?' And the old man would answer, 'What kind of people lived in the place where you came from?' If the travellers answered, 'Only bad people lived in the place where we came from,' then the old man would reply, 'Continue on; you will find only bad people here.' But if the travellers answered, 'Only good people lived in the place where we have come from,' then the old man would say, 'Enter, for here, too, you will find only good people.'

When we encounter those who behave badly, we must remember that we, too, have acted badly at times. If we wish for others to forgive us, should we not also be open to forgiving them? Those who habitually behave badly need our compassion for they may not have been given the circumstances or tools needed to evolve beyond that behaviour. We, too, may be looked upon by others as being crude at times – or all the time for that matter. Too often we cannot see ourselves as others see us. Many a misunderstanding would be avoided if we had this awareness.

Aikido shows us our commonality: our common laughter; our common sorrow; our common puzzlement; our common discomfort; our common condition. It enables us to see that, given the right circumstances, the monk can fail and show his shortcomings while the thief can be noble and show his compassion.

Of course, no matter who you are or how saintly your actions and words, there are always going to be situations where people take offence when none is meant. The point is that we can never hope to fully control someone else's perceptions. What we can do is work to change our own, while allowing and adjusting to others. If we can do that, then we will begin to find peace.

9 • FINDING AN AIKIDO TEACHER

*True budo is a work of love. It is a work of giving life to all
beings, and not for killing or struggling with each other.*
— Morihei Ueshiba

Finding an Aikido school and a credible Aikido teacher may
be a formidable task, depending upon where you live. The
reason is that in Aikido, unlike most other martial arts where
black belt is given out in as little as a single year, it can take
many, many years to reach black-belt level, let alone receive
certification as a recognized Aikido instructor. If you do find
such a certified teacher, count yourself fortunate. If you live
in a large city, there is a greater chance of there being one or
more Aikido *dojo*. And as the number of reputable *dojo*
increases, so does the probability of having access to an offi-
cially certified and sanctioned Aikido instructor. Some
people even go so far as to move their geographical location
in order to train with certain Aikido teachers. Naturally this
action should only be considered after quite a bit of research,
research that is best accumulated after spending some time
training in a local Aikido *dojo*.

If you plan on staying in your area, one of the quickest ways
to determine if there is an Aikido school near you is to check

the phone book's advertising listings. In the US, for example, this would be the 'Yellow Pages' section under 'Martial Arts Instruction' or 'Karate Instruction' and it would be under 'Martial Arts' in the UK. Aikido schools that are large enough to warrant the cost will probably advertise themselves here.

Some *dojo* post flyers or brochures around town, such as in local health food stores, sporting goods stores or the like. Word of mouth is often a good way of finding out about a good *dojo*. Talk to friends and others about your interest in Aikido, and you may find someone who knows where you can train.

You can also contact the larger Aikido *dojo* and organizations, Aikido periodicals or the Internet for help in locating a *dojo* closer to you. You will find a couple of these listed in the back of this book.

Once you have located a school or schools, call for class times and to arrange a visit. Politely enquire what Aikido rank the instructor holds, when and from whom it was received and, if applicable, the source of his or her certification. You could also enquire about the instructor's teacher, where the instructor trained and for how long. Additionally, check what affiliations, if any, they may currently have with recognized established Aikido organizations.

When visiting, get a feel for the spirit of the *dojo*. Some of the best *dojo* may not look particularly pretty. Although this could be a sign of apathy, don't be distracted if they are on the right path. People are attracted to Aikido because of Aikido; the look of *dojo* is less important.

Meet the chief instructor, if you can. Be polite and courteous. It is considered bad manners to approach them personally, though, with questions about their own credentials. You should not interview them, but that does not prevent you from getting a sense of them and their character. Traditionally, of course, you are the one being interviewed. It is you who seeks potential membership in the *dojo* with hopes of being accepted as a student of this teacher. You should handle yourself accordingly.

Observe the students both on and off the mat. Do you feel they are of good character? After all, these are the students you will be practising with and learning from as well. Does the overall atmosphere have a safe feeling? In that, I mean, does safety play an important role in what is going on in the training? Some teachers prefer a feeling of danger and uneasiness to better bring out a serious focus in their students. Some insist on such a safe environment that no one feels challenged. In the latter, a true sense of accomplishment and assuredness may be more difficult to instil and maintain. Nonetheless, it may be a perfectly valid *dojo* in which to study some of Aikido's other aspects, without the prospect of potential injury that can be present in the tension of a more physically perilous training atmosphere.

There are *dojo* that may allow you to take a sample class before committing to join. Then again, others recommend you watch class as often as you like, but require you to commit to membership before being allowed onto the mat. If you visit a *dojo* that will not allow you to watch class unless you join, be very wary. If a *dojo* has a children's class and does not allow parents to be present – walk out.

Certainly, personal recommendations by people you trust can lead you to a qualified teacher and a good school. Ask around: a little networking may well lead to tracking down a school. Some *dojo* are small, do not advertise and are known only by word of mouth. Be careful. Because of Aikido's increasing popularity, there are many other questionable martial artists seeking to cash in on the public's unfamiliarity with reputable Aikido teachers. A little knowledge can be a dangerous thing, and some of these impostors have little or even no training in traditional Aikido. They may not hesitate to call themselves experts when, in truth, the real experts would never make such a claim. Like most arts, the best Aikido teachers and *dojo* are the ones solely dedicated to Aikido. Depending upon the particular teacher, either a more martial or a more esoteric aspect of Aikido may be emphasized. That emphasis may even fluctuate between the two and, to various degrees, from class to class and even moment to moment.

Some stress severe practice – 'on the edge' training – while others prefer to focus on gentle interaction. Some recognize the benefits of both and encourage exploration into both. All are valid; it is one of the reasons Aikido is so universally appealing. People are attracted to its varied aspects for any number of reasons. The one common underlying factor is a desire for peace. There can be many approaches and individual expressions of Aikido. That is part of Aikido's ultimate appeal. Although some people may prefer Italian food to Chinese, to those who prefer it, Chinese food still provides nourishment. To invalidate Chinese cuisine simply because you don't like it is absurd. So it is with various teachers of Aikido. Their methods and their styles may be disagreeable to you, but keep an open mind. This does not invalidate their work and the learning of those who are attracted to their teaching.

Traditionally, in most of the martial arts, nothing was really 'taught' to students, at least not as we think of it in the West. The teacher demonstrated what had come from time spent in the art, and it was up to the student to 'steal' the technique. The student had to use all his senses and abilities to grasp the essence of the technique in its purest form – without verbal reliance – and to ingrain it deeply into his core through practice, repetition, and trial and error. This often meant, and still does in *dojo* that prefer this traditional way, that those who could get it, do; and those who could not, don't.

As aikido continues to spread to other cultures, other teaching methods are brought in by individual teachers wishing to better facilitate and explain the art to the masses that are attracted to it. This includes balancing verbal instruction with the visual and physical. Because of this accommodation and versatility, aikido principles are now taught in corporate and institutional environments to people who will never perform an *iriminage*, the trademark entering throw of aikido or, for that matter, step onto an aikido mat.

When seeking an aikido teacher, respect your own instinct, intuition and gut feeling, as well as your own life experience. If the teacher and school inspire you – if you feel the right path is being travelled – then ask, humbly and respectfully, if you can join. If you do, I wish you good luck and peace throughout the journey.

CONCLUSION

I hope that this book, in some small way at least, has helped you to understand better the beauty of Aikido. If you want to know more about the art, there follows a reading list that I highly recommend. Aikido is immense. There is no way possible for any one book to contain it. So – explore.

In writing this book one of my favourite quotes comes to mind: 'It is better to keep your mouth shut and be thought the fool, than to open it and remove all doubt.' Well, I've broken that rule here, but I have done so with the hope that I may have helped you. Thank you for your time and the opportunity to talk with you. Maybe I'll see you on an Aikido mat soon.

GLOSSARY OF
JAPANESE TERMS

Since Aikido was created in Japan it naturally uses Japanese terminology. This glossary will cover the most common basic Aikido terms. There will be, according to various teachers and styles, slight variations in terminology, but on the whole the following terms are generally recognized throughout the art. Some entire concepts are contained within them, and this makes their continued use both practical and convenient.

Aiki	*ki* harmony
Aiki-jo	weapons practice (staff)
Aiki-ken	weapons practice (sword)
Aikido	the way of harmony with *ki*
Aikidoka	practitioner of Aikido
Aikikai	Aikido Organization/Foundation
Ashi	foot movement
Bokken	wooden sword
Budo	martial ways
Bujitsu	martial combat
Chudan	middle position
Dan	black belt
Do	way, also refers to the torso
Dogi	uniform for practising the way
Dojo	place where the way is practised
Doshu	leader of the way

Fudoshin	immovable mind
Gedan	low position
Gi	training uniform
Go	five
Gokyo	fifth teaching, fifth technique
Hachi	eight
Hakama	traditional pleated skirt
Hanmi	stance
Hanmi Handachi	kneeling techniques done on standing partner
Hara	lower abdomen, spiritual center located here
Henka Waza	switching from one technique to another
Hidari	left
Hombu Dojo	Home *Dojo* (of Aikido)
Ichi	one
Ikkyo	first teaching, first technique
Irimi	entering movement
Irimi Tenkan	enter and turn
Iriminage	entering throw
Jiyu Waza	freestyle techniques
Jo	wooden staff
Jo Tori	weapons disarming technique
Jodan	high position
Jojutsu	jo (staff) arts
Ju	ten
Jujinage	crossed-arm technique
Kaeshi Waza	reversal techniques
Kaitenage	rotary throw
Kamae	basic ready stance
Kamiza	place where the spirit of the *dojo* sits
Kanji	brush calligraphy
Katame Waza	pinning techniques
Katate-tori	wrist grab
Katatori	shoulder grab
Keiko	practice
Keiko Gi	practice uniform
Ki	spirit/energy/life force
Ki No Nagare	flowing techniques
Kiai	shout with harmonized *ki*
Kihon Waza	basic techniques
Kohei	junior
Kokyu	breath power
Kokyu-ho	breathing method

Kokyunage	breath throw
Koshinage	hip/waist throw
Koshita	lower back plate
Kote	wrist
Kotegaeshi	wrist turnout
Kotodama	study of sound
Ku	nine
Kumi Jo	two-person *jo* practice forms
Kumi Tachi	two-person *bokken* practice forms
Kyu	various ranks below black belt
Ma-ai	distance/time
Men	head
Migi	right
Misogi	purification
Morotetori	two hands grabbing one arm
Mushin	empty mind
Musubi	blending
Nage	defender
Ni	two
Nikyo	second teaching, second technique
O Sensei	Great Teacher
Obi	belt
Omote	in front
Randori	multiple attack practice
Rei	to bow
Roku	six
Rokyo	sixth teaching, sixth technique
Ryotetori	two hands grabbing two hands
San	three
Sankyo	third teaching, third technique
Satori	enlightenment
Seiza	seated, kneeling position
Sempei	Senior
Sensei Ni Rei	bow to sensei
Shi	four
Shihonage	four direction throw
Shinzen	*kamiza*
Shodan	first-degree black belt
Shomen Ni Rei	bow to the shomen (*kamiza*)
Shomen Uchi	overhead strike to the top of the head
Sichi	seven
Sojutsu	spear arts

118

Suburi	basic solitary strikes
Suki	opening, opportunity
Sumi-otoshi	corner drop technique
Suwari Waza	kneeling techniques
Tachi Tori	weapons disarming technique
Tai No Henko	body adjustment
Tai Sabaki	body movement
Take-musu aiki	unlimited purification and renewal through *aiki*
Tanden	one point, center located just below the navel
Tanto	knife
Tanto-tori	knife disarming techniques
Tatami	traditional Japanese floor mats
Tegatana	sword hand
Tenchinage	heaven and earth throw
Tenkan	turn
Te no uchi	hand gripping movement
Tokonoma	alcove for reflection
Tsuki	punch
Uchi	strike
Udegarame	arm containment technique
Udekimenage	arm projection
Uke	attacker
Ukemi	falling ability
Ura	behind
Ushiro	from behind
Waza	opponent
Yokomen Uchi	strike to the side of the head
Yonkyo	fourth teaching, fourth technique
Zanshin	mindfulness

FURTHER READING

Crane, R and K, *Aikido in Training*, Cool Rain, NJ, USA, 1993

Crum, Thomas, *The Magic of Conflict*, Touchstone, NY, USA, 1987

Dobson, Terry, *Aikido in Everyday Life*, North Atlantic Frog Ltd, CA, USA, 1993

Dobson, Terry, *It's a Lot Like Dancing . . .* , North Atlantic/Frog Ltd, CA, USA, 1993

Fields, Rick, *The Awakened Warrior*, Tarcher/Putnam, NY, USA, 1994

Gleason, William, *The Spiritual Foundations of Aikido*, Destiny, VT, USA, 1995

Heckler, Richard Strozzi, *Aikido and the New Warrior*, North Atlantic/Frog Ltd, CA, USA, 1985

Homma, Gaku, *Aikido for Life*, North Atlantic/Frog Ltd, CA, USA, 1990

—— *The Structure of Aikido*, North Atlantic/Frog Ltd, CA, USA, 1997

Klickstein, Bruce, *Living Aikido*, North Atlantic/Frog Ltd, CA, USA, 1987

Leonard, George, *Mastery*, Dutton, NY, USA, 1991

O'Connor, Greg, *The Aikido Student Handbook*, North Atlantic/Frog Ltd, CA, USA, 1993

Pranin, Stan, *Aikido Masters*, Aiki News, Tokyo, Japan, 1993

—— *Aiki News Dojo Finder*, Aiki News, Tokyo, Japan, 1996

—— *Aiki News Encyclopedia of Aikido*, Aiki News, CA, USA, 1991

Saito, Morihiro, Saito, *Aikido, Its Heart and Appearance*, Minato, Tokyo, Japan, 1975

———— *Takemusu Aikido* Vols 1–3, Aiki News, Tokyo, Japan, 1994

———— *Traditional Aikido* Vols 1–5, Minato, Tokyo, Japan, 1973

Saotome, Mitsugi, *Aikido and The Harmony of Nature*, Shambhala, MA, USA, 1993

———— *The Principles of Aikido*, Shambhala, MA, USA, 1989

Shimizu, Kenji, Akidio, *The Heavenly Road*, edition q, Tokyo, Japan, 1993

Shioda, Gozo, *Total Aikido*, Kodansha, Tokyo, Japan, 1996

Siegal, Andrea, *Women in Aikido*, North Atlantic/Frog Ltd, CA, USA, 1993

Stevens, John, *Abundant Peace*, Shambhala, MA, USA, 1987

———— *Aikido, The Way of Harmony*, Shambhala, MA, USA, 1984

———— *Invincible Warrior*, Shambhala, MA, USA, 1997

———— *The Essence of Aikido*, Kodansha, Tokyo, Japan, 1993

———— *The Secret of Aikido*, Shambhala, MA, USA, 1995

———— *The Shambhala Guide to Aikido*, Shambhala, CA, USA, 1996

Tesoro, Mary, *Options for Avoiding Assault*, SDE News, CA, USA, 1994

Tohei, Koichi, *Aikido in Daily Life*, Rikugei Publications, Tokyo, Japan, 1966

———— *The Book of Ki*, Japan Publications, Tokyo, Japan, 1976

———— *Ki in Daily Life*, Ki No Kenkyukai HQ, Tokyo, Japan, 1978

———— *The Book of Ki*, Japan Publ. Inc., Tokyo, Japan, 1997

———— *What is Aikido?*, Rikugei, Tokyo, Japan, 1962

Ueshiba, Kisshomaru, *Aikido*, Hozansha, Tokyo, Japan, 1974

———— *The Spirit of Aikido*, Kodansha, Tokyo, Japan, 1984

Ueshiba, Morihei, and John Stevens, *The Art of Peace*, Shambhala, MA, USA, 1993

Ueshiba, Morihei, *Budo in Training*, Sugawara, Tokyo, Japan, 1997

———— *Budo*, Kodansha, Tokyo, Japan, 1991

Westbrook/Ratti, *Aikido and The Dynamic Sphere*, Tuttle, Tokyo, Japan, 1970

Yamada, Yoshimitsu, *Ultimate Aikido*, Carol Publishing, NY, USA, 1994

USEFUL INFORMATION

Aikido Journal: Aikido periodical, published in Japan; selected Aikido videos and books.

For those interested, an exceptional video series on O Sensei is available, some of which show him demonstrating his *kotodama* chants. These videos showing O Sensei performing Aikido have been wonderfully and expertly compiled by the editor of *Aikido Journal*, Stan Pranin. *Aikido Journal* has also produced a series of articles and interviews concerning the Omoto-Kyo religion for those interested in the spiritual influences and beliefs of O Sensei.

Aikido Journal also addresses Aikido historically related arts such as Daito Ryu *jujitsu*, *aikijitsu* and sword arts, among others. *Aikido Journal* publishes a yearly *Aiki News Dojo Directory* containing Aikido *dojo* listings around the world.

Subscription information:
Aikido Journal
USA Office
Aiki News
50-B Peninsula Center Dr. #317
Rolling Hills Estates, CA 90724
USA

Editor: Stan Pranin
e-mail: ajmag@earthlink.net
Tel/Fax: 1 310 265 0351 (USA)
Tel: +81 427 48 2423 (Japan office)
Fax: +81 427 48 2421 (Japan office)

Aikido Today Magazine: Aikido periodical, published in the US; Also offers a catalogue of Aikido videos and books.

This is an excellent source of information for those interested in Aikido, and in the United States in particular. *Aikido Today Magazine* also publishes a fairly comprehensive Aikido book and video catalogue. Each issue also contains a list of current Aikido seminars.

Aikido Today Magazine also supplies a yearly updated list of active Aikido *dojo* both in the *Aikido Today Magazine Dojo Directory* and on-line at their web site.

Subscription information:
Aikido Today Magazine
c/o Arete Press
PO Box #1060
Claremont, CA 91711-1060 USA
Tel: 909 624 7770
Fax: 909 398 1840
Editor: Susan Perry
e-mail: atm@aiki.com
home page: http://www.aiki.com (contains an international Aikido *dojo* directory)

AUTHOR INFORMATION

Web address:
www.aikidocenters.com

Email:
greg@aikidocenters.com

Mailing address:
Greg O'Connor
Aikido Centers of New Jersey
301 Millbrook Ave.
Randolph, New Jersey 07869
USA
Tel: 973 898 9858
Fax: 973 328 2828

INDEX